AWAKENING TO INFINITE PRESENCE

ROBERT WOLFE

The completing volume to *Living Nonduality*
and *Abiding in Nondual Awareness*

Karina Library Press
2015

Awakening to Infinite Presence: The Clarity of Self-Realization
Robert Wolfe

ISBN-13: 978-1-937902-23-0

Library of Congress, LCCN: 2015939952

Manuscript preparation, Katherine Holden.

Cover: detail of artwork by author.

Karina Library Press
www.karinalibrary.com
PO Box 35
Ojai, CA 93024

Michael Lommel, Publisher
michael@karinalibrary.com

Other books by Robert Wolfe

Living Nonduality

Abiding in Nondual Awareness

Always—Only—One (on the Ashtavakra Gita and other texts of India)

One Essence (on the Hsin Hsin Ming)

The Enlightenment Teachings of Jesus (on the Gospel of Thomas)

Science of the Sages (on science meeting nonduality)

Elementary Cloudwatching (a journal)

The Heart of Living: The Heart Sutra (ebook)

Contents

"...inside my little room
there plunged the rays of Love...
out of which the Nameless makes
a Name for one like me...
and I was tumbled up
in formless circumstance...
my room it looked the same—
but there was nothing left between
the Nameless and the Name."

—Leonard Cohen (in the song *Love Itself*)

"These forms we call 'you' and 'me'
are only the surface we see.
And though Love came
wearing your name
it's omnipresent, now, and free..."

"So drown me in your darkest pain,
your softest kiss, your sweet despair.
I've seen Your face now, and I know your name,
and I can find you *anywhere*."

—Lyrics of singer-songwriter Kirtana

Preface

As with *Living Nonduality* (first published in 2009) and *Abiding in Nondual Awareness* (five years after), this is a continuing exploration in the territory of experiential nonduality, also known as spiritual awakening. Like the other volumes, many of these monographs were written in response to queries, from seekers of Self-realization. There are included here several longer discussions, of imperative matters, which space didn't permit before.

Since each monograph was written independently of the others, there is unavoidably some repetition; but each was chosen for its variation of expression of the multiple facets in a profound paradox.

The material was organized to be read consecutively, with earlier discourses amplifying later topics.

– RW
Ojai, 2015

Introduction

"I am awake."
– Buddha, speaking of his enlightenment

It is recorded that someone came to Ramana Maharshi and said, "I understand that you can give enlightenment."

Ramana replied: "Yes. I can give it. Can you take it?"

The age-old precepts which are known as Self-realization are not difficult to understand. Upon awakening, an aspirant will sometimes exclaim, "It's so simple!" Or, "This is it!" Or, "It's right *here*. Now!"

Many more, who are aspirants still, lament: "I've had a glimpse of the underlying reality, but somehow I've lost it." Or, even more commonly, "I have an 'intellectual' understanding of nonduality, but I feel there's something about it I'm still missing."

It's one thing to understand the implications of the spiritual teachings, and another thing to apply them to our worldly circumstances with consistency.

The ancient word for remaining in existential confusion is "ignorance"; that is, to not be aware of what it is that one can be aware of.

What is to be known, in the instance of Self-realization, is an amazing paradox. It would not be too fanciful to say that spiritual awakening can make our worldly life seem to be an optical illusion. And this is because what we're searching for, in terms of ultimate reality, has always been everything that we *see*. And that includes ourself.

So, when we ignore this part of the teaching—and leave ourself out of the equation—we are bound to entertain incomplete, and inconsistent, conclusions.

As Ramana said, "Can you take it?" When the nondual teachings clarify that you (as you suppose your self to be) and the phenomenal world (that you take to be real) are illusional appearances, will you merely find that an "interesting idea"? Or, are you open to this realization radically altering your values, and the way this temporal life is lived?

When Buddha said, I am *awake*, he wasn't confusing his realization with an "intellectual understanding."

Self-Realization in three words: the I-thought neutralized.

The writings which follow can clarify, for the sincere aspirant, elements of the nondual precepts which often tend to be overlooked, or not given serious enough attention. The paradox of enlightenment is that the ultimate reality, which we search for, is *inescapable!* That makes it too *simple* for most people.

What You Really Want?

In 1988, the person who knew himself only as Robert Wolfe was subjected to a sudden "spiritual awakening" (a term that is more directly descriptive than "enlightenment"). Since that time (for nearly 26 years, at this writing), that which knows itself as Robert Wolfe by name/form only—"I"—found just one activity to be at all meaningful: "transmission of the dharma," as the Buddhists call it. That is, attempting to be of assistance to those who sought a fundamental shift in awareness, called Self-realization.

In that endeavor, I have experimented with several forms of communication. Of these, I have found the most effective to be "one-on-one" discussion with interested individuals. Over the years, I have spoken with many dozens of persons on this basis. Of these, I would estimate 3 in 10 have (it seemed clear to me) directly benefited by grasping the essence of the message.

These discussions tend to unfold in a familiar pattern because the basic strata of our spiritual confusion is our common societal conditioning. I, too, had been a subject of that common societal conditioning, so I have had first-hand acquaintance with the condition of spiritual confusion that persists in the absence of Self-realization. An incisive communication evolves as a natural consequence of the experiential meeting of minds on common ground.

Then, let us—you and I—have a one-on-one discussion here and now.

This *search* for a shift in fundamental awareness is a consequence of those "I" or "me" related questions which begin with "what" or "why"—such as "Why am I here, in this world?" or "What is my life all about?"

We do not ask these questions in a vacuum: generations that have gone before us have offered answers to these "cosmic" questions, as a result of their own discoveries. They have generally suggested that each individual is a *limited* expression of a holistic, interconnected reality. This is a view that we seem to intuit in any attempt to make sense of our personal existence, generally expressed as a feeling that we are "part" of something "greater" or more extensive; that there is an intelligence which transcends our individual consciousness, or may be the underpinning of our consciousness.

And there is something which suggests to us that it is important, perhaps vital, to know more about what this is; that it may, in fact, reflect on our actual form of being. If there is more to us than meets the eye, what is "it"?

This "it"—unknown something—has taken on various names, among many cultures. And the quest for the discovery of "it" has, by individuals of every age, taken many forms.

One of the forms it has taken in our contemporary society is that of the inquiring individual (such as Robert Wolfe in the 30 or more years leading up to 1988) who personally sets aside time to read the writing of legendary enlightenment teachers or exemplars, or to attend talks, listen to tapes and CDs, and watch videos and DVDs of various spiritually-centered figures who are alive today. In this self-activated quest, we hope somewhere, somehow, to uncover the truth which reveals the mystery of that unknown something— the "it"—which we long to know first-hand.

16

And it is in this meeting—between those who are seeking, and one who sought and now no longer seeks—where the exchange begins.

The first important question to be asked, though surprisingly simple, is: "How would you describe what it is that you are looking for?"

It is usually an inquiry which the aspirant has never verbalized, even for her own benefit. But it is necessary that the discussant have a clear understanding of what is being referred to. If I say "it" but "it," to you, means "peace" or peace of mind, while to me it means "the unknowable," we are not even in the agreement of context.

Sometimes the "description" offered will be "the indescribable" or some similar noncommittal designation. The question, then, to be asked is: "If that which you are looking for is indescribable, where do you suppose that it is to be found?"

Sooner or later, the aspirant will describe verbally what "it" is that is being sought, in terms of what it is that is presumed to have been found, or discovered, by others. In a word, it will be that which has been described as holy (a derivation of "whole"), sacred (revered), divine (deity), or some other definitive word for that which is traditionally regarded as "both immanent and transcendent," or the so-called "first principle."

The next question to be asked (and no less important) is: "What do you expect will happen when you've found 'it'?"

The object of a search is the conclusion of the search. A search is undertaken because of a conviction that its conclusion will result in a consequential change. What is the change which is expected to occur when there has been a sought-after encounter with the noumenon?

Historically, this anticipated change has been called enlightenment, realization, awakening. And, by whatever term, the implication is that this condition will have a significant (even profound) effect upon the life of its discoverer. Expectations of what this effect entails may range from annihilation to bliss, from fear to anticipation.

Again, few aspirants have asked themselves this question, or defined clearly what their expectations include, in relation to this potentially life-changing discovery. If the response is, "I don't know," or "I don't have an expectation," the question is: "If you do not have a supposition of what to expect, how will you know if you've found 'it'?"

The concluding question may seem unnecessary, by this point, but it is a denouement of the first two reflective questions. "Are you prepared to make that discovery today—regardless of your expectations?"

Obviously, there is not much point in pursuing into the exploration if there is not an unambiguous affirmative response to this query. And, for some persons, the prospect of the meeting of the "unknown"—here and now—evokes an evasive or negative response. The immediate life-altering quality of enlightenment is well attested, and not everyone has come to a time and place where they are committed: "Is this what I really *want*, or am I merely curious about this subject?"

This question also makes it clear that what is to be discovered may have no relationship to the suppositions, or expectations, identified in the first few questions.

Neither the revelation of the enlightened condition, nor its consequent effect, may bear any resemblance to one's prior conceptions of it. This may, to some, be viewed a relief, to others a disappointment. The question is, in the pursuit of the "unknown," are you truly prepared to meet that potentiality right now, without equivocation? A salutary enquiry.

From here, the discussion can proceed to examining the fundamental confusion which obscures Self-realization. And the questions that were asked earlier have a bearing on the underlying confusion.

The first question, in this deeper exploration, begins to sort out the basis of the confusion: "What does the word 'relative' mean to you?"

Relative, obviously, refers to a relationship between two or more things. The definition for each relative item is conditional on the definition of each other item. My aunt is my relative because I am her nephew. The word aunt has no meaning apart from the meaning of the word nephew. Each relative item is dependent for its meaning—actually, its existence as a thing—on what it is not: cold is cold because it is not hot. That which is relative has *reality* only in comparison to some other (relative) things.

The most obvious and elementary example is "you" and "I," both relative terms: I am me because I am not you; if I were you I wouldn't be me. So, clearly, each individual has an existence which is relative to (all) other individuals. Individu-ality is a relative condition. To say "me" or "you," or "this thing" as contrasted to "that thing," is to speak in relative terms.

And this, of course, is the substance of our conditioning. From the time that mother points to herself and says "mama" and then points in the crib and says "baby," we begin to think in relative terms. This becomes so much of a habitual perspective that we never even question whether there is any alternative to the relative, or relational, mindset—the inter*dependent* existence of this thing as opposed to that thing; man at one end of a spectrum, for example, and nature at the other end. The relative perspective is at the root of our conception of all things that we suppose to have existence, including our self and others.

So, the next query is: "For that which is not relative, how would you describe that?" That there is a condition which we describe as the relative suggests that an alternative condition may exist. Supposing that is true, what might the non-relative be? If it is not "this thing" or "that thing" (or, relatively, any "other thing"), then it must be something which has no relationship to relative things—it must be beyond, or above, relativity in any of its forms: non (not) relative.

If It is not to be found (definitionally), for example, in the form of "man" (this—relative—thing) nor the "world" (that—relative—thing), then it must transcend ("go beyond") these forms—which are limited by reason of their relative definitions.

By contemplating the definitional meaning of that which is non-relative, it is possible for a pivotal insight to be present. Let us look at this in more specific terms.

Any form, or forms, which we identify as an entity unto itself—which is the purpose of every word that we use—is a relative conception. "You" are a form, an entity, relative to "me." In our (conditioned) perspective, we presume these forms, or entities, to be two "different" things: individuated. Even if we connect the two things—you and I—as "we," the form of we is simply relational to that which is definitionally not-we: "they."

So, anything we speak of as singular is merely an oppositional concept, relative to the plural: "one" and "many" are both relative forms.

An alternative term for relativity is duality. The habituated, relational mindset out of which we operate is a dualistic perspective: perceiving reality in terms of two—or more—forms; there is me, for example, and there is God. There is (a form of) good, and there is (a form of) evil. There is love and there is hate. These are dualistic conceptions, the consequence of that relational perspective which has dominated our pattern of thought throughout our life.

An alternate term for non-relative is *non-dual*: "not two things." The penetration of the meaning, the significance, of nonduality presents an option to the limited, and limiting, perspective of dualistic conception.

That which is non-relative, or nondual, transcends all that is relative: by definition, the non-relational can have no relationship with, or to, any thing: in particular, any thing which is relative—which all "things" are.

The nondual, therefore, is not simply the opposite of dualism; it has no oppositional (or any other kind of) relationship. If it were merely the counterpart of duality, it would be *relative* to duality.

What this means in practical terms is that nonduality is not the negation of duality: to be so, it would be in relationship to duality. As an example, nonduality is not the joining, or combining, of two (dualistic) forms—or more—to create one uni-fied form. "I" *and* "you" are still "we": all are relative forms. The nondual is a condition *transcendent* of "I," "you" and "we" (*or* "they"). It "surpasses the limits" (the meaning of transcendence) of all forms, because all forms are relative, and limited to their individuated entities.

So, the nondual is not in the form of "two," nor is it in the form of "one" (which is relative to two).

The most meaningful way of considering this is that dualism is equivalent to separation, or separatism. Each (dualistic) form is an entity unto itself, either in its singularity or its multiplicity. A person is a form; trees are also forms; each is consequently a separate entity; and all are relative to each other. My dictionary contains 150,000 words: each word divides our reality into a separate category, each—whether referring to the material or the immaterial—describes a different form.

While nondual is also a word, its implicit meaning is "non-relative," transcendence of all relationship. There is a more explicit word which precisely defines such a condition: absolute. Its definition: "wholly unlimited, completely unrestricted; not dependent on anything else, not relative." So the absolute is not dependent upon any relationship to duality for its condition, or reality. It is not at the opposite end of the spectrum from the limited relative; being beyond limitation, it is transcendent of dualism. Therefore, the absolute is beyond being (or not even) an entity, beyond being a form. As such, it does not even represent what is conceived of as "one," its condition could be said to be "nothing," no thing.

Due to our ingrained dualistic thought process, the significant meaning of the absolute is normally overlooked. But it has a profound bearing on the enlightened insight.

While the relative represents all that is limited to form (and the separateness that defines each form), the absolute—beyond form—is *without limitation*. By virtue of its unlimited condition, it surpasses, transcends or *encompasses* all that is finite (formed) or limited, within its presence or existence. In other words, while the limited cannot contain the unlimited, the unlimited has the capacity to contain, or include, all that is relative. The absolute represents *entirety* in the sense that there is no thing identifiable *beyond* it; it defines reality in the most *comprehensive* or ultimate way possible.

Comprehending the significance of the meaning of nonduality, as represented by the term absolute, brings us to the brink of the investigation into the mystery which enlightenment has traditionally revealed. When the aspirant is prepared to look beyond the limitations of the conditioned dualistic perspective, a revelation is possible: the consideration not of a thing—not even "one thing"—but of *no-thing*.

It is no mystery, then, why the word absolute (usually capitalized) is an alternate term for that which every spiritual tradition—in their own lexicon—designates as Supreme Being, and characterizes as divine, sacred, and so forth. When the opening question is asked—"How would you describe what it is that you are looking for?"—some variant of the descriptive words for the ultimate cosmic reality surfaces, sooner or later.

The Absolute (by whatever of its myriad parochial names) is evocative of the *infinite* and *eternal*; surpassing any limitation whatsoever spatially, and beyond any conceivable restriction in time. As such, it describes the endless and timeless condition beyond which no finite or temporal form or reality prevails. As the essence of *being*, it is the matrix from which all origination and development proceeds, and into which all impermanent entities recede. Therefore, it is the quintessence of the complete, the whole (thus its derivative "holy"), the totality of an unfathomable, awe-inspiring cosmic unicity.

Needless to say, the above description (of that which, by its unlimitableness, its ultimately beyond description) is the universal characterization of the invisible presence or reality that in every spiritual tradition is identified as the Absolute, and regarded reverentially. And it is a direct and immediate immersion in the totality of this presence which the aspirant instinctively seeks.

What then are the clues given us as to the means of the discovery of "it," if that is a possibility?

(As shorthand, I will utilize for "it"—or the Absolute, or other of the superlative names—the generalized term historically used by advaita [nondual] sages, or teachers: That. Granted, the word "This" would be more evidently appropriate.)

In every spiritual tradition and by sages regarded as enlightened historically, the description that most commonly characterizes That which is absolute is "omnipresent."

The significance of this term is that it means a condition or presence which exists "in every place, at all times simultaneously." Always ever present, illimitable in duration or location.

If there is any possibility that there is any such reality as that which is perceived to be omnipresent, there are revelatory implications concerning the means of its disclosure.

The first peculiar property or characteristic of that which is omnipresent is that it evidently would be thoroughly indivisible. Any division or fragmentation of its presence anywhere would allow it to be separable into parts or elements detached in space or by time. But entirely unrestricted by time or space, there could pertain no boundaries by which it was confinable. An absolute *omnipresence* admits of no partitions, as an essential quality.

And, more significantly, by virtue of its indivisibility, it could not be present in anything less than its whole undiminished entirety at any and every point in conceivable time or space. Pinpoint any quark in the cosmos, in other words, and the Absolute would be completely and unbrokenly *present*—as it would simultaneously also be, in any and every other quark—without any barrier superior to its all-inclusive scope.

Its profound qualities are even more self-revealing. Being unconstrained by any finite limitation or boundary of any kind, an absolute omnipresence would not only encompass or surround every existent form or entity in the cosmos, it would also permeate or saturate every conceivable thing. This is precisely what is indicated by the appellation that is also traditionally applied to the all-inclusive Absolute:

that it is equally transcendent and immanent; perceivable everywhere in general but also anywhere in particular, whether focusing *internally* or *externally*. In language that echoes back as far as the Vedas, the strongest clue is lodged: "There is no where that It is not." At any and every point in space and time, the Absolute is indivisibly present, without exception.

This also leads to some of the other mysterious qualities that have been ascribed to the Infinite. As the non-relative cosmic plenum, itself void of form, all existent forms originate or manifest in the potential of its presence. So, it has been remarked that each and every relative thing situates "within" the Absolute—while simultaneously the Absolute is inhabiting impartially, and *itself undifferentiated*, "within" each and every relative form.

The Absolute, being the only *permanent* reality by virtue of its nature as eternal, can be regarded as the *essence*—the intrinsic, indispensable element—of all relative, impermanent existence. Therefore, it can be perceived to not only be present around, in and through all that is, but essentially "as" all that is. In other words, as the sages indicate, the Absolute is the *fundamental* "identity" of all that we otherwise identify by differentiating names.

Consequently, at the most elementary level, there is no separation anywhere of any thing, material or immaterial, by reason of spatial distance or temporal transit. Not one quark in the cosmos is disconnected from any other, across space or by time. Not anything lies outside of the all-pervasive ever-present condition that is defined by the Absolute. If it were possible for It to exist "apart" from any thing, that would clearly be in negation of the significance of its omnipresence, as the nondual or non-relative. It does not even exist as a separate form or entity that can be termed such things as Spirit or Godhead, because of its formless quality. It can only be identified as the innate or inherent essence that is transcendent of every form or entity and of all limiting terms, such as "relative" *or* "non-relative." Even the word *That* is intended to point to "all that exists." Apart from the identity of all *things*, It has no special identity of its own.

The comprehension of this incomparable dynamic can be the catalyst for a profound "spiritual" realization. It is the underlying principle in the advent of instantaneous enlightenment.

That which the aspirant seeks exposure to is the essence, the manifest identity, of everything which exists, whether corporeal or incorporeal, formed or formless, individual or collective, separate or unitary: not anything in the cosmos is excepted. It permeates, saturates, every atom, ion, particle (and their enclosures or partitions), to generate one whole, unbroken, infinite and eternal existence. There is no time which bars its presence; there is no point in space, or in matter of any kind, which bars its presence.

This cosmic presence cannot be anywhere other than right *here*—no matter where "here" is. And it cannot be anywhere other than right *now*—no matter when "now" is.

Being beyond confinement, it is not "close" to you, it penetrates and permeates your very form; it is not "inside" of you or "outside" of you, it is as much what comprises you as the "self" that you suppose you are. And it is the essence of your existence right here, right now. You have not ever, in any way, been in the least apart from it; nor has any other thing or being been apart from it/you.

There are, in fact, no separate "parts" in the interconnecting wholeness of the Absolute, nothing "individual" which stands outside of its inclusiveness. All things which *appear* to be individuated are merely multiple extensions of That.

This makes it clear that—as a so-called individual; as "you"—you cannot discover the Absolute reality as a condition apart from yourself. You and That are the same simultaneously existent reality. The startling discovery is that not only can you not pursue That, you cannot for a moment *escape* it.

When this is clearly and fully recognized, it is apparent that there can be no "encountering experience," in terms of a special mystical event. The much-anticipated, long-awaited epiphany is actually a brief, quiet, simple shift in perspective from the one who is looking for That, to the recognition that it is That which is looking.

This is why the second question—"What do you expect will happen when you've found It?"—needs to be addressed. The aspirant's seeking leads her to suppose that she will somehow encounter the Absolute, and that she will be merged in it. This expectation is based on obfuscating presumptions: that the "individual" form or entity will *unite* with a "higher" form or entity (or even formlessness) which is exterior in its existence. However, the revelation is that there is no individual which has ever been *apart* from the all-pervading Absolute. What is "expected" to happen is already a present reality; not any thing is separable in any way from the omnipresent. By looking for it outside of every thing which is already here and now, the seeker misses it perpetually!

And this is why the third question is equally worthy of attention: "Are you prepared to make this discovery today—regardless of your expectations?" The moment of awakening, the "experience" of enlightenment, is simply a direct and immediate *realization* that the self which recognizes itself as That, is That reifying its infinite, indivisible existence: *self* awareness, in the most divine respect.

In order for the Absolute to express its true identity, its "true nature"—even *to*, or by, its Self—it must be recognized to be all that is; not some entity or abstraction somehow or somewhere difficult to locate or appreciate or sense: not *a* Supreme Being, but *supreme being.*

The deeply-felt recognition that the Absolute is all that is, and consequently that must include you, is the life-changing substance of enlightenment. All things are That, you as well as all other human beings: there is only That, in the sense of ultimate, permanent reality.

How, then, does one live one's life when the present awareness is "I am That, and all else is That"; when the perception of being a "separate individual" has dissolved, and the ego (Latin for "I") is no longer at the center of one's perspective?

"Real-i-zation" (the "enlightenment" the aspirant has sought) means "to make real." How do we make the real— the essence of timeless reality—the central expression of the Absolute perspective we have now discovered to be inevitably our own? To "make real" in one's life and activities the awareness that "all that is, is That" is unavoidably a life-altering engagement. Are you prepared to "live" with this discovery today?

So, the real question, the final question, is not "How am I to come to Self-realization," but "Is enlightenment what I really want?"

> *This* we have NOW
>   is not imagination.
> *This* is not grief or joy
>   not a judging state,
>   or an elation or sadness—
> Those come and go.
> *This* is the PRESENCE
>   that doesn't!
>
>   – Rumi

Bedrock

There is a perception which, once realized, gives lasting peace of mind. This perception is that all phenomena in the universe are the manifestation of an "energy" which is not—nor has ever been or will ever be—in any way divided.

There is a universal energy which is completeness in constant change. It is not, and cannot be, contained; its movement is not limited by time or space. Because it is unlimited, it is without beginning or ending. It is completely and constantly whole: this energy is everything which is.

It is present in every place, this very moment—and this present moment is the only actual time there is. It is the "movement" of this energy which makes the moment endless, which makes it the endlessly changing moment that it is.

There is nothing which *shares* this energy; all things *are* this energy. The energy is indivisible. Because everything *is* this energy, there is not anything which is separate, apart, from all else. "You" have never been—and never will be—severed from this energy; nor have you ever been, or will you ever be, isolated from all else that is.

You are not presently a "part" of anything, because there is not anything that you have ever been disjoined from. Since you have never been apart from all else that is, there is no "self" which can actually have been formed as a separate part. The self does not exist, except in the human imagination; there is no "part" of the universe which can, in reality, be distinguishable from the remainder of the universe. You are this energy, and this energy is boundless and in constant transition…uncontainable within such a fixed confine as man's conception of the "self."

Man is the "unhappy" animal. And the self is a fiction of man's mind; it is the creation of conceptual thought. The viewing of things which are *different* as being somehow *divided* from all other things is a quirk of our imagination— whether what is considered as different is "me," "you" or "it"; whether it is defined as special, foreign or merely unusual; and whether it is thought to be a concrete reality or an ephemeral event.

Division, like the self, is solely a concept, a notion. Where there is no such notion as division, there is not such a notion as the self.

When your perception of this is complete, contention will be replaced by tranquility. This is something which will not be taken away from you. It is the bedrock.

Em-bodi-ment

Since my own awakening 25 years ago, I've had many dozens of discussions on Self-realization, one-on-one.

What has been of great help to me in these discussions is that I've talked, written or read about this subject probably every day, for a couple of decades.

In terms of the reading, it's ranged from ancient classics to current publications. One thing that you notice, when reading enlightenment material, is that these teachings have been refined over the centuries. Look at the Vedas, and the difficulty the writers had in describing these matters. Even from a generation ago, the teachings of people like Alan Watts or Krishnamurti are being refined by spiritual teachers today.

The most common concern that spiritual teachers hear—and you can hear this on CDs and DVDs, in the question-and-answer period—is: "I have an intellectual understanding of nonduality, but I don't feel that I'm quite there yet. Is there something I'm missing?"

To have an intellectual understanding is better than having no understanding at all. But, in many cases, what these persons are stumbling on is a common matter that has to do with what follows realization, and that's what some teachers call "embodiment"—living out of the precepts, beyond merely awakening to them.

The spiritual aspirant is seeking to be one with ultimate reality. Every spiritual and religious tradition has used in common a particular word to describe ultimate reality (or what is otherwise called God, the Absolute, Brahman, Tao, etc.): omnipresent. *Omni* is Latin for "all"; *present* has both a time and a place sense to it, and the inference of "existing before being referred to." The Latin is a combination of "before" and "essence." So, omnipresence infers "that which is in existence in every time and place." And there can only be one such thing, because any *other* would obviously occupy the *same* existing time and space.

Thus, if you stabbed a pin, anywhere in the universe, into the air or into an object, the pin point would connect with the omnipresent. And if you reversed the pin and stuck it into your body, your brain, eye, tongue, etc., you could not avoid contact with omnipresence.

Hence, the reason why omnipresence is used to indicate the ultimate reality is because there is no thing in existence which *restricts* the presence, or being, of ultimate reality. Not anything, material or immaterial, can be outside of the omnipresent. Therefore, the ultimate omnipresent reality must be where *you* (and all beings and objects) now are, outwardly as well as inwardly.

This is the meaning of the Vedas' "Tat Tvam Asi," That (ultimate being) *thou* art. In other words, every human being's utterance of the word "I" is issued from an organism totally immersed *in* and saturated *by* That. This unimpeded omnipresence inter-connects all of existence in the universe, in an unbroken, inseparable whole or one-ness. The word *essence* means "essential; that which anything cannot be without" or apart from; and not anything exists unimbued with this illimitable essence.

The significance of this, in terms of spirituality, is that our "essential nature" is not only the context in which we come into *being*, but also the context in which we *act* as individuals. The word *spirit* means "life force," and it is out of (or a consequence of) this ubiquitous life force that we think, speak, and do. So, when you recognize that there is only one ultimate reality and that it is the essence of all that exists, you realize that all that is thought, said, or done anywhere is attributable to this singular life force. This is exactly what is meant by the Gita's teaching "*You* are not the doer of any of the deeds that are done." Put another way: You are *That*; and That is what's doing whatever it is that you suppose that you do—or say, or think, as well.

When a seeker has come to recognize that, in a spiritual sense, "he" or "she" is superseded by a universal presence which eclipses our personal individuality, the seeker is said to have "awakened" to true nature. The nature of that revealed truth is that all is essentially one; while simultaneously that *one* is inherent in, and *expressed* in, all. In short, as the scriptures say, "There are no two things"— which is what "nonduality" means. With this intuited self-realization, one's seeking ends.

However, upon this point of discovery, a concomitant insight needs to be availed.

The major teachers of Advaita—such as Ramana Maharshi and Nisargadatta, and going back to Shankara—were from a different culture then we are. In the West, ours has always been Judeo-Christian. Even people who consider themselves to be atheists often don't realize how heavily we are all conditioned by Christian concepts. Only 47 verses into *Genesis*, you have the idea of the tree of the knowledge of "good and evil." The notion that something is good and something else is evil was not a common idea to every society, when this was written. We, here, have been conditioned to this premise, since our infancy.

Who, among us, does not have an imagined spectrum, or scale, in the mind, with "negative" at one end and "positive" at the other. Every experience that we have, we mentally assign a value on this scale, as somewhere toward the "good" or the "bad." And our cultural heritage supports the idea that we should continually be moving everything from the negative end of the scale toward the positive.

The consequence of this dualistic disposition is that our every aware thought is in terms of what we conclude *should* be happening, as opposed to what we declare *shouldn't* be happening.

There's also another consequence. What "should be" and what "shouldn't be" are prejudicial ideas concerning "what *is*." This *idea* is what results in *idealism*: if we can move the what-is to what-should-be, that would be ideal personally. "I should be perfect"—somewhere off the scale, above "positive." Even more ideal: "*You* should be perfect." Where this leads us is away from the moment of *being* what we actually are, to some hoped-for distant moment when we—as a human—will be something no one has ever been.

This is what is referred to in the spiritual teachings as "becoming," versus *being*.

For the spiritual seeker, this future ideal is often associated with enlightenment: "Some day, I am going to come into contact with ultimate reality, and live in an enviable state of unending bliss. Never again will I know a negative thought, a moment of anger, a lustful desire, and so on."

So, here's where the rub comes in.

Someone I am speaking with describes what they characterize as an "intellectual" understanding of the precepts of nonduality. But what I am hearing them describing is that they have awakened to the truth of their true nature, as the teachings of Self-realization consistently portray it.

Upon this discovery, whether it was dramatic or not, there was a period of relief and ease and awe. But all things change: even in enlightenment, observed *phenomenon* come and go.

Somewhere, in the daily life, this person notices a moment of anger, a judgmental thought, or a negative reaction. And their conclusion is: "I must not have gotten the message, or I've lost it. This occurrence shouldn't be happening!"

This is simply a matter of not yet fully *integrating* the awakened perspective.

These teachings are telling us to *transcend* the dualistic spectrum, with its right-and-wrong, better-or-worse, good-versus-bad polarities.

Self-realization, when embodied, or acted from, is "to *be* present with what is present"—good, bad or otherwise: whether or not the what-is happens to be what you presume it *should* be.

And here's the kicker. Even when you are present to your moments of not reveling in clarity, you are nevertheless continuing to be present with what *is* present. Enlightenment is not some idealized fixed state of perfection.

One of the books of Ramana's teachings takes its title from his admonition: Be As You Are. Not as how you imagine a saint is supposed to be.

When you are free to *be*—and at peace in *being*—who you are, that's the embodiment part.

In a Moment

There's one thing in common to all seekers: the conviction that what is not being seen is not present. With all who seek holding this *presumption*, it tells us that herein lies a key to ending the search.

The seeking ends when it is recognized that what's been sought is already fully present.

What is already always present? The present moment.

But the seeker unavoidably stands, body and mind, *in* the present moment. So, what's the hitch?

This all-too-common, ordinary moment isn't what the seeker's quest is focused on. The searcher is intent upon discovering an extra-ordinary moment.

The irony is that nothing can be more extraordinary than when it is perceived that this present, unexciting moment is the moment which we come to realize *is* the very moment we've been awaiting!

Freedom is not stationed months away, waiting for you to discover it. Peace is not holed-up in a distant time zone, hunkering down until you buy a plane ticket. Those who wake up, do so in the exact moment they are in.

Everything in this immediate moment, material or immaterial, is pointing to the place and time where enlightenment reveals itself. When you ignore it, you'll be in the next moment. And it will be there too.

The difference between seeking and not seeking is only one moment.

Simple Enough?

Indra:

The irony of Self-realization is that it is so *simple* that we try to make it into something more complicated than it is.

It can be (and has been) summarized in three words: Tat Tvam Asi; That thou art. The "That" means the Absolute, the Omnipresent, Brahman, or whatever name you choose to represent the infinite and eternal, the actuality which is both imminent and transcendent. Some call it God.

"Thou" means the body-mind organism which seeks to be aware of its true ("divine") nature—or "you," as a "seeker" of "spiritual" truth.

The three words say—adequately—that the seeker, "me," and the infinite Presence are not two *different* "things," but are the same, "one" thing in essence, in *actuality*— however otherwise it may *appear* to be.

This is *all* there is to Self-realization—to *realize*, consciously and thoroughly, that "you" cannot possibly, in any way, be *apart* from Omni-presence.

However simple this is, and for whatever "mysterious" reasons, there are people (seekers) who go throughout life without inculcating this (rather *obvious*) realization. One of the possible reasons for this is that this simple (and reasonable) proposition is not complicated enough for them; they refuse to accept that the truth can be so immediately evident.

I Am That, Nisargadatta titled his book; meaning, the all-pervading Presence and that which is aware of its self as "I" are ultimately *identical*: not *separable*. When the awareness of a body-mind has comprehended that it is, in fact, an expression (as are all other things) of the One "mind" (as Buddhists call it), it is clear that the seeker and the Totality that is sought are *already* "united."

Therefore, there is no point in ritually repeating any phrase to yourself; nor to continue to cling to *ideas* (read or heard) about what one needs to do to *become* united. You cannot possibly be apart from that of which the enlightened say, "There is *nowhere* It is *not*." That means It *is* where "you" *are*.

So, "who" is this "me," under the circumstances? I *am* That; the body-mind organism is That; and the organism's *awareness* is That. Hence, even if it were possible (or necessary) to "get rid of the 'me,'" as your question suggests, what would be left? Since "all that is, is That," *whatever* was left—would *still* be that! In other words, whether a "me" is present or a "me" is not present, whatever *is* present is That omnipresent actuality—in any and all cases.

So, recognize (as you say) that "the me is always here": but, "who"—ultimately—*is* that "me"...none other than That. This is all there is to *Self realization*; self and Self are One and the same. Non-dual: "not two."

Not two. Not two. Not two.

Sudden or Gradual?

Enlightenment is not like a retirement fund, in which there is an accrual that in time will dependably reach its goal. Even if you have had a spiritual practice for forty years, the realization which occurs as undeniable clarity occupies but a moment.

It is in the wake of this *Aha!* moment that the *gradual* phase begins. This is a matter of getting accustomed to, or acclimated to, a radical shift in one's perspective. Values will change, attitudes change, and behavior changes. Developing over a greater or lesser span of time, depending on each participant's maturity, Self-awareness will be finally embodied.

So, the *sudden* part is the advent of knot-cutting Self realization. The *gradual* element is the living out of the Absolute awareness which has dawned.

Yield: "Give in Return"

To open a door is one thing; to step through the door is another. Spiritual truth opens a door, and what is revealed can inform one's life in astounding ways. Exposure to the basic principle of cosmic inseparability can have immediate and profound impact on the components of normal human suffering and anxiety. Personal psychological conflict and strife can drop away virtually overnight.

But there may, perhaps, be a degree of difference between a psychological revelation and a spiritual revolution. *Psyche* basically refers to "mind," and *spirit* refers to "breath." The breath is ephemeral, formless, dispensable—never gained back in the same way it was given.

The psychological benefits of a spiritual inquiry (such as "peace of mind") are manifold—and ever-presently accessible. This element is generally the particular attraction for those whose primary concern is the cessation of their private agony. Some find it possible, up to a point, to alleviate the tension of profane existence without having to significantly reorder their circumstances or to surrender any of the private ground previously "gained."

But the full breath of spirit is similar to the ocean: what you scoop up is proportional to the capacity of the vessel you bring to the beach. In other words, the bounty is there—as much as you apply for. The critical element is not so much the size of the vessel, but how empty it is for reception.

Emptiness (in this context) can be equated to surrender (in another context). To surrender means "to give up; yield," whatever completely yields all content is empty. To yield all content, in this context, would be to surrender to the "spirit." It means to penetrate beyond one's personal, psychological contentment and satisfaction.

It means not merely opening an expansive door and peering in awe within; it means stepping through the door. This has sometimes been likened, in spiritual writings, to "falling into the Void." It is to move, without resistance, from the known to the unknown. Since all that we normally know is temporal worldliness, it is to leave the mundane world behind. And this is not meant to seem entirely metaphorical. An acquaintance, nearing death, refused medication: her doctor said, "Are you prepared to die today?" In spiritual terms, that becomes more than a rhetorical question.

"Awakening" and "illumination" are synonymous descriptions (and synonymous occurrences). It is not illumination that lights *your* way, it is illumination that lights *the* way—through the unknown, one step at a time.

It's not a freedom to locate personal contentment. It's the freedom to cross each bridge as we come to it, and to watch it burn behind us—without dismay. It is to be open, exposed, vulnerable; it is to face one's very worst fears from moment to moment, without lingering.

There is no one, who ever lived, who did not eventually surrender all: some while they could yet experience the freedom. While enlightenment is often considered to remain tantalizingly in the future, surrender is an apparent (all too apparent) possibility *now*.

In following the uncommon light, however, one lives an uncommon life. To go where you have not been before, you have to leave completely where you've been. And you cannot know, for certain, what awaits you there—pro or con.

Said of a life committed to spirit, by Jeff Dietrich:

> *It is not a job. It is a vocation. It is a prodigal, prolifigate, wasteful adventure. It is an adventure in which you get to give away everything, expecting nothing in return.*

Glimpsing It

"I've had glimpses of the Presence you write about, Robert. But I haven't yet had the experience of being fully and lastingly in touch with that Reality."

Nonsense. Where could Reality, or Presence, be hiding from you? With your eyes wide open, look around you right now, wherever you are. What you are seeing is exactly what Buddha himself would be seeing. It's the present *reality*! Not only what you are seeing, but what you are hearing, feeling, thinking, doing, or aware of—that's Reality. What you are "glimpsing" right *now* is Reality.

You *are*, whether you realize it or not, "experiencing" Reality. And for Reality to make itself even more boldly plain and obvious, the experienc*er*, the glimpser itself, is present *as* Reality.

How much more "fully and lastingly" can you be in touch with Reality, than to recognize that even when you are *not* aware of it, you cannot ever even *escape* present Reality.

What you are looking *for*, is everywhere you look—or *don't* look! Either way, you are "experiencing" Reality.

Discovering True Nature

There is a simplified way to understand nondual teachings. The word *form* means "shape" or "image": a human takes a form; a thought, or a plan, is formed. Each form is limited within the bounds of its definition, its particular function. Each *thing* is a form which is distinguishable from similar things. We might speak of some thing as: an activity; or a quality; or a symbol; or a concept, etc. Each thing has a relationship to all other things, even if it is just that it is not the same form. That there appears, to us, to be more than one form is what is termed *duality*. *Adam* and *Jehovah* exemplify duality.

Forms have their source. We say that thoughts, plans, concepts, images take shape in, or are generated from, a mind. We know that the source of the materials that compose the planets arose from remnants of our solar system. A *source* is "that from which some thing derives."

Things which *have* being (have come into existence as formed) arise from a *condition* of being. This condition of being, which produces existent forms, is not a form like the multiplicity of forms it is the source of; the continual *plurality* of forms, which appear in every place and time, arise from a *singular* state of being which is not confined by space or limited by time.

In other words, things arise from a presence of being that is not itself just another thing: forms arise from a source that is formless; finite forms owe their existence to a presence of being which is not finite, but infinite—unconstrained in space or time. Being illimitable, there is not anything outside of it, thus apart from it; it is all-inclusive. All that exists, or will exist, is within it. The source of all multiplicity is itself indivisibly singular, or *non*-dual.

Forms return to this ground of being from which they originated. The dualities, impermanent in time, ultimately dissolve into the nondual source of finite existence, the infinite ever-present.

What this tells us is that the forms and the formless are merely aspects of an unbroken, inseparable actuality. There is not, at any point, a severance or disconnection of the *many* from the *one*, nor the one from the many. The forms appear within a greater whole or totality; they are *appearances* of the nondual infinite as its finite, and impermanent, expressions. The shapes and images do not appear, or exist, independently of their permanent, or eternal source.

Thus, the nondual perspective, or teachings, allow us to put *our own* forms in context, in terms of ultimate reality; in terms of what is timelessly true or vital.

All that you know *your self* to be is nothing but a form—finite, impermanent. The source from which it "comes" and to which it "returns" is formless, without beginning or end in time or space. That, the teachings say, is your *true* nature.

World Premier

The world is real.

A dream is illusion.

The world is a dream.

On the relative level, even the sages admit that there is a concrete world which appears to our senses, and which provides sustaining nourishment to our body.

Yet we all recognize that in a dream—which has no substance or permanence—we *also* sense the appearance of a concrete world, and dream food satisfies dream desire.

When we awaken from a period of sleep, the dream world vanishes, along with every character who seemingly had a relationship to that world.

And so, when our sensory consciousness shuts down in death, this real world will disappear as if merely imagined, along with seven billion characters who had appeared to be in relationship to it.

In fact, even the universe—in which all this was composed—will retain no more reality for you than if it had been a movie projected on a screen.

Eat your popcorn, meanwhile, and enjoy the plot.

Thought for the Day

In 1972, a physics experiment proved that two subatomic particles, once linked, would experience an instantaneous, simultaneous effect on each other, even if light-years apart. In 1990, further experiments demonstrated that this supernatural phenomena occurred also with three particles, which had originated from the same source before spatial separation.

A recent book by scientist Amir Aczel, Ph.D., (*Entanglement*— the physics world's word for this discovered feature) recounts the details of these, and related, experiments. He summarizes the significance of the experiments:

> "Entangled entities (subatomic particles, such as photons) are linked together because they were produced by some process that bound them together in a special way....And such photons (or particles), produced in a way that links them together, remain intertwined *forever*.

> "Once *one* is changed, its *twin*—wherever it may be in the universe—will change instantaneously.... Notions of 'causality'...are shattered...But entanglement is even more dramatic, for it breaks down our notion that there is a meaning to spatial separation. Entanglement can be described as...two or more particles, taken as *one system*....

> "Two particles that can be miles, or light-years, apart may behave in a concerted way: what happens to one of them happens to the other one instantaneously, regardless of the distance between them....Entangled

particles transcend space. The two (or three) entangled entities are really parts of one system, and that system is unaffected by physical distance between its components. The system acts as a *single entity*."

Matthew Fox once noted: "The hydrogen atoms in your body were created 14 billion years ago." Considering that quantum particles are constantly interacting, is it likely that any of them are *not* interlocked, over a period of 14 billion years?

And what becomes of these particles once they no longer comprise your body? Hydrogen atoms are in the fluids of your body, and are interchangeable with the hydrogen atoms in all bodies. They are found in every water in the world, in every breath of air that anyone ever breathes.

Are the particles of which you—and all others—are composed to be "taken as one system," a system that "acts as a single entity"? Is your entanglement in this system one of short duration, perhaps a hundred years, or might it "remain intertwined forever"?

The Field of Actuality

We exist, physically, in a universe where there appears to be the difference of opposites; male and female, life versus death, hot or cold, profit and loss, etc.

Each opposite, in any pair, is dependent upon its counterpart for its existence or definitive identity; for example, anything which can be said to have a beginning must be said to have an ending.

These inseparable counterparts are connected by a continuum. The darkness of midnight is at one end of a gradient that has the brightness of noon at its other end.

Both extremes tend to be neutralized at some median point where their definitional ranges merge. A ledger might show neither a "profit" nor a "loss" but a "break even" figure.

Each of these contrasting conditions is in relation—that is, *relative*—to another. We say that something is "alive," to the extent that it is not "dead." Designating any point along the continuum of these two opposites (for example, to assert that something is "nearly dead") is to operate within the context of what is called "duality."

Probably the most common expression of duality is the perspective of "me" in relationship to "you"; or, collectively, "we" as opposed to "they": at one, separate pole are "these" humans, at another pole are "those" humans.

The dualistic perspective can involve any two—or more—particulars: me versus you; me and god; god versus you, etc. (or me, nature and god; me and you versus nature; you, love and god, etc.)

Any proposed relationship of any two or more subjects or objects is a "dualistic" equation.

So, that which is relative depends upon its connection, or comparison, to some other thing. And, because of the *contrast* between the two things, the relationship between presumably "separate" entities is said to be dualistic.

In the physical world, the relative or dualistic framework is our usual and continual point of reference. However, if it is our only, or invariable, context for reference, it will be the source of a stupendous confusion.

Notice what happens. From our normal perspective of dualism: if there is anything in this universe that is not relative, it would have no meaning or significance for us unless we contrasted or compared it to what is relative. And so we would place the "not-relative" in juxtaposition to the "relative," in order to be in relationship to it.

However, when we place the "nonrelative" in a relative position, it is inadvertently no longer—by definition— *non* relative.

Put another way, if there is anything (in the realm of possibility) that is not relative, it must therefore *not be relative* to anything that *is* relative!

For the sake of clarification, let us substitute the word "absolute" for "non-relative." This is the purpose for which the word *absolute* was intended; it means "not relative or limited; complete, whole."

However, if we unconsciously slip back into our normal dualistic perspective, even the distinction of the word *absolute* will be lost in *relational* context. "Absolute" is *not* the *opposite* of "relative."

The meaning would, by definition, not be absolute if "absolute" were limited to a relative position to an "opposing" word.

The key point here is that anything which is limited to the relative scale is not free to take a position equivalent to the absolute.

And here is where the usual context, of dualism, falls short: the absolute, not being in a position *relative* to *anything*, has no *limiting position*. That is why the Absolute and the Infinite (when capitalized) are traditionally utilized as synonyms for the omnipresent reality.

The Absolute, maintaining no particular position, is unopposed. Being itself without limitation, it encompasses all things unto itself. This is why absolute is also defined as "complete."

So, while something that is limited to the relative cannot encompass the limitless Absolute, the Absolute—by definition—encompasses everything that is relative.

Put another way, when relative limitations dissolve, the Absolute (if anything) remains.

To cast this in a different light, when our usual dualistic perspective is suspended, there is the prospect of a non-dual, limitless, "absolute" or unitary perception.

Phrasing this graphically, each person has the freedom, at any time, to perceive from either a "horizontal," polarized perspective or from a "vertical" unitary perspective.

But while the perspective from the absolute can accommodate the context of the relative, the relative perspective cannot accommodate the nonrelative essence of the absolute.

For the sake of discussion, let us call the "apex," or the vertical meridian, the Universal. Our definition will include the previous designations: nonrelative, absolute. While the noun *universe*—Latin: "(to turn) all together"—is commonly used as a synonym for our cosmos, that is not our primary meaning here. The fundamental definition of the adjective *universal* is "present or occurring everywhere; unlimited, unrestricted; entirely applicable without exception." And, so, we are stressing its sense as *infinite*, rather than as simply *cosmic*.

In this sense as infinite ("everywhere present"), the Universal is the essence of all that is. Therefore, there is not anything that it is in opposition to. It is not relative to any other thing, since it universally permeates any other thing that it might be considered relative to.

Since it is absolute—permeating all things throughout infinity, and is not separate from anything—we cannot even (properly) call it "oneness," because it is not a unit or entity or element separate unto itself. While this Universal absolute is not *two, neither* is it *one*.

In other words, this Universal (or Absolute) is not a condition in which the dualities (such as polar opposites) join together and become one. The Universal—which is not limited to any relative position, and thereby is "present everywhere without restriction or exception"—already permeates the apparent dualities (such as polar opposites) *before* they could even be brought together into unity.

The infinite, nonrelative universal Absolute is omnipresent ("everywhere at once"). It is, by definition, anything which we could possibly describe as "relative" *or* "nonrelative"— or at any point on the continuum between; or even beyond.

In the fullest sense of the word, the Universal is really *actuality*. The definition of actuality is: "not merely possible, but in fact; present existing condition." Actuality, omnipresent, *is* 'what is'.

If there is something which is *relative*, that is what is. If there is anything which is *nonrelative*, that is what is.

The 'what is' can be relative or non-relative (or any condition in between); but whatever truly *is*, is actuality.

And, so, the perspective of the vertical meridian can be called the Nonrelative Absolute, the Infinite Universal Essence, the inseparable Omnipresent Actuality—and will likely continue to be called such things as Oneness, Unity, God, etc.

The point is that as long as a person persists in adhering fixedly to the dualistic perspective (that is, on the "real" rock-bottom "plane" of the relative), the perspective of the Absolute is obscured. One sees "things," rather than what might be called "the thing." One looks at a basket of apples and recognizes only "many"; he chooses the most proximate apple and recognizes only "one"; he does not recognize that whether he samples one or many, they are essentially "the same."

But the person who is capable of incorporating the Absolute perspective, of "seeing beyond" the relative identity of particulars, is enabled to accommodate *either* dimension of reality.

To give a limited, thumbnail example of this, if my perspective is that of the relative world, I will probably consider that the pendulum of life's possibilities fluctuates between the extremes of my "happiness" or my "unhappiness." In order to achieve a condition of harmony, or balance, I might manage to maintain a state of equilibrium: neither happy nor unhappy.

But my constrained equanimity is still nothing more than the median point on the continuum; my "being centered" *depends* upon not gravitating toward happiness or unhappiness.

In other words, happiness, unhappiness and equanimity are merely interchangeable manifestations, emanating from a singular source—me. But while the outward manifestations vary, that which manifests them—me—remains the same, singular source.

From the perspective of the Absolute, the perception would be that there is only "one thing" (in the sense of its inseparable omnipresence), and that it is the essence of "all that is." Therefore, whether we choose to refer to "me," "happiness," "unhappiness" or "equanimity," we are ultimately referring to one, indivisible actuality. (Nisargadatta called it That, Alan Watts alluded to it as It.)

So the realization would be that "I am It," "happiness is It," "unhappiness is It," and "equilibrium is It."

Therefore, whether there was an awareness (on the relative scale) of happiness, unhappiness or any contrasting condition, the transcendent perspective would be, "That, too, is It!"

The point is that one need not attach oneself to any inflexible position. You can operate in the world of relative "reality," or you can operate in the universe of quintessential actuality.

The latter *includes* the former. But the former *excludes* the latter.

To the extent that there is a relinquishment of your myopic relativity, you are free to choose.

But the ultimate realization is that there is not any*thing* to choose.

Getting to Know Ramana

David Godman is perhaps the best "interpreter" of Ramana's teachings (in English), editor of *Be as You Are: The Teachings of Sri Ramana Maharshi* (Penguin paperback). A good place to start. It's 244 pages include a glossary and index. Don't skip the Introduction.

The late Arthur Osborne was a Western student of Ramana, and edited *The Collected Words of Ramana Maharshi* (Weiser Books paperback). Not a lot was written by Ramana himself, and Osborne explains much about what was. Again, don't skip the Preface. The 192 pages include glossary and index. Ramana wrote in Tamil, and many references are to Vedanta.

These are good preparation for *Talks with Sri Ramana Maharshi*, the major source for his direct teachings; some 650 brief, transcribed Q-and-A on many topics (with students or with visitors) over about four years (late 30's). 640 pages, hardcover, with extensive glossary and index, it is best read with the above preparation. A thorough Bibliography, at the back, will lead you to choices of the many other books, of many sorts, to follow with.

Now in its 13th printing since publication in 1955, *Talks with Sri Ramana Maharshi* was produced by Maharshi's ashram in India. From 1935-39, a disciple acted as a recorder of Maharshi's dialogues with visitors—somewhat like journal entries. Maharshi was evidently well-read in classical Indian spiritual literature (*after* his enlightenment), so—in speaking frequently to Indians—he often used Sanskrit phrases.

While earlier editions of the book had only a 10-page glossary, and a 24-page general index, it now has a 42-page index—with each Sanskrit indexed word followed, at the same location, with its definition. In addition, there are 33 pages of categorized indexes to assist in locating a passage you only recall, making it a more useuful resource. Otherwise, it's the same, original text (and now available at Amazon.com).

Sri is an honorific, similar to Sir; *Bhagavan* is a title given to holy persons, similar to Blessed. Devotees referred to Sri Bhagavan Ramana Maharshi simply as Bhagavan; the book uses "M," as an abbreviation for Maharshi.

M was about in his mid-50's during this time. The significance of Maharshi's life and teaching is that spiritual aspirants need not reinvent the wheel. In terms of spiritual experience, it is evident (as one can recognize in reading a biography of Maharshi) that he has "been there, and done that." Among the visitors, just during these four years, were Somerset Maugham, Yogananda, Tibetan scholar Evans-Wentz, writer Paul Brunton, Maurice Frydman, swamis, muslims, the Maharajahs of Mysore and of Travancore, Indian congressmen, Brahmin pandits, and philosophy professors.

Among the many that sat in M's presence each day were those caught up in the traditional concepts of established religions (Hindu, Christian, Muslim, Buddhist, Theosophy, etc.)—such as 'reincarnation'. Then there were the scholars who treat enlightenment as an academic subject and want to clarify scriptural terms. There are, of course, those who come in quest of occult and mystical powers. And there are inevitably those who appear with a "problem"—men and women alike.

There are many who want instant dispensation ("grace"; shaktipat), by the guru tapping their forehead or whispering a mantra in their ear, as if being enlightened by an ATM machine.

Practically every entreaty could be summarized, "Tell me, what is realization? And how may I attain it?" Since the listener usually resists thinking "outside the box," M's teaching is plain, simple and direct; the listener—who would like as long as possible to continue in his or her worldly ways—often ignores his direction and asks instead if M can recommend some "practice" that can be pursued toward the same ends "meanwhile."

M is realistically pragmatic. He judges the state of spiritual maturity of his listener (often by the question) and responds accordingly. Answers are always keyed to the level of the listener's comprehension. If a person insists on asking about karma, M begins by quoting some of the things that are said in the spiritual literature about karma—but which are invariably misunderstood. He may then comment pointedly, "Karma is as real as the individual."

M's responses are almost predictably repetitive, because he had one succinct message. And generally he used the term "Self" (which the scribe capitalized) to refer to the Absolute, to stress the point that absolute *Self* is the same as the *self*—individual—with a small "s". But he also used "Brahman" with Hindus, "God" with Christians, etc. And he sometimes used "I-I," indicating the One "I" that is at the *same time* the individual I.

He generally spoke in reference to himself as a *Jnani*, which defines a Self-realized sage. Its counterpart, a person who has not realized his true nature, is an *ajnani* (a- indicating "not").

The Word is not the Thing

During the couple of years that I lived at a Zen retreat, I was sometimes amused at the difficulty some practitioners had in distinguishing the Zen precepts from the overlapping Japanese culture.

Illustrative of this: While the principles of Zen Buddhism have no necessary relationship to a steady diet of brown rice eaten from a bowl with chopsticks, on the few occasions when someone prepared pancakes for breakfast, our Jiki-do (sangha director) insisted that we eat them out of a bowl—with chopsticks.

And so it is, likewise, with the teachings concerning advaita: some people exhibit confusion between what are the nondual teachings and what are Hindu cultural (or even superstitious) expressions.

The point is: you do not have to know a single thing about India, or its traditional belief systems and mythologies, in order to come to a realization of your own true nature.

Fortunately for many seekers in the West today, there are Self-realized teachers who are capable of winnowing the wheat from the chaff. If you encounter a teacher who can't make sense in the normal language which we all understand, patiently look elsewhere.

> *"If you can't explain something simply,*
> *you don't understand it well enough."*
> – Albert Einstein

Un-becoming You

In order to function in life, a certain kind of mechanical knowledge is necessary. This type of knowledge is based on demonstrable fact: "This is an automobile, this is a gear shift; if I turn on the ignition, put the gear in Forward and press on the gas pedal, the car will move forward." Like tying your shoestring or walking, once the brain has assimilated this knowledge, the thinking process comes into play for the activity without your even needing to be aware of it.

But the brain is also capable of a more speculative kind of thinking, which is more conscious and not dependent on fact. This is the type of thinking—imagining—that we do primarily throughout our day: "Jim and the boss are talking...probably about that new project...it could mean we're going to start on that today."

Without making a distinction in our mind, we normally recognize both types of mental activity simply as "thinking," and the process in either activity as "thought."

However, there is a subtle difference in the results of the two activities. When we think thoughts that are based entirely on facts, we normally draw factual conclusions, upon which we can act (whether our facts are correct or incorrect): "So, if I put the gear shift in Forward, the car will move forward; but I can't go forward, where I am parked; so I will need to go backward...put the gear shift in Reverse."

If our thoughts are of the speculative type, we may *also* act upon our conclusions, *even though* our conclusions are not dependent on fact: "If we're going to start on that project today, I'd better go for an early lunch—so that I'm back when they're ready to get started."

Aside from making a mistake—which usually is reversible—we seldom have problems as a result of our mechanical knowledge. But our speculative knowledge normally builds one speculation upon another, and—in directing our actions—leads us in confusing directions: "But if I'm out at lunch when they're ready to start, the boss will get mad. Jim would just love that! I think I'll skip lunch."

Speculative thinking becomes most dangerous to us when it is involved in abstractions. Abstract means "to drag or draw something away." Abstractions are conclusions which need not be dependent on fact. They are usually the result of making comparisons between what seem to be related things: "Jan was once charged with shoplifting; Doris has never been accused of theft, so far as I know; I think Doris is a relatively honest person, compared to Jan."

These comparisons cause us to form notions: "Jim was a good friend of the boss' wife; when Drew retired, Jim was given Drew's office. It's not what you know, it's *who* you know that counts!"

Notions become beliefs and ideals: "The United States is the most progressive country in the world"; "Anyone who would not die for this flag is a traitor to mankind"; "Old Glory is the banner of freedom, world-wide." Beliefs and ideals are at the core of our emotions: "I go into an uncontrollable rage, when I see someone burn our flag"; "Glenda and I were together for fourteen years, and I just can't keep from crying every time I think of how she betrayed me"; "I never thought I could be angry at God—until Denny died!"

Perhaps the notion which has become the most troublesome to us, and has led us in the most confused directions, is the idea of time. There is a function that the knowledge of time has, on a mechanical level: "I am going to drive from Whitesboro to Amity, which usually takes three hours; therefore I will have to start out at nine to be there by noon." This is the time of the clock; factual time. Then there is the *concept* of time; speculative time: "I am alive at this moment; I was alive a moment ago, and I might be alive in the next moment. I will agree with others to refer to the previous moment as the *past* and the pending moment as the *future*."

The concept that there is any other time which *exists*, other than this actual moment we are aware of, is just that—a concept. There is no place in reality where you can go, nothing you can do (even imagining in your thoughts) that is *actually* in the Past. We have arbitrarily agreed, as a convenience for communication, to divide the perpetual movement, of all time, into three conceptual categories: past; present; future. When, exactly, is the Future? It's relative; there is no such thing, except in relation to something else.

This psychological concept of time— as opposed to the mechanical reality of seconds, minutes and hours on the clock (or sundial or hourglass)— allows us to form a concept of our self. If there was no conscious time but the moment (which has no identifiable beginning or ending), there would be no self that existed "before"…or will exist "after."

The entity of the self (or any other selves) we "know," is dependent on thought—in the same manner that any past or future we know is defined by thought. We "know" what "we" did in the "past," because thought (stored now in memory as "knowledge") carved out the existence of a past, as well as the notion of an entity (which presumably resides in this body as a person-ality) called the "self." Once our mind has told us that we have a separate self, and that there is (somewhere) such a thing as a past and a future, we can— in our thoughts (stored as memory)— interact with "our" past.

When we combine our notion of self and our notion of the existence of time (time that is dependent on our conception of it) with the mind's ability to create abstractions—and then to compare them—we have another concept known as *becoming*. Be-coming: "about to happen"; not actually happening, but predicated to happen in the relative future. "I am this; I should be that. I will *become* that." *This* moving to *that*— in time.

By comparison with others, I judge that I am unhappy; I decide that I would prefer a different abstraction: to be happy. I determine that if the self makes some effort over a period of time, I will move from relative unhappiness to relative happiness. The psychological self will go from one psychological place to another psychological place, given the proper amount of time: "I will become happy."

In many cases, we presume that we will *become* as the *result* of an experience (also predicated to happen over some period of time): "I am not sure that she loves me; when Gloria and I finally make love, I will know that she cares deeply about me."

The notion of *becoming*—through time, including the time of "experience"—sets in motion the motivation of ambition: "I am going to do this thing; I am willing to pay the price to do it. Now I just need to determine the best way to go about it." A search, a mission, is underway. The end result of a search is to find something, to locate something. That which is found, if anything, is the reward for the search. We have set out, taken our risks, and as a result we have "gained" something. (Or, if we haven't found what we search for, we have "lost" something—at least the time involved.)

Ambition (which is an expression of the ego, or "center" of the self) posits that the self—which is lacking something—will achieve, or gain, something. If, however, the self does not gain what it set out for, the self is *still* lacking something. This is a disturbing, uncomfortable prospect for the self—which deemed that it lacked something worth taking risks to gain. As far as the self, the ego, is concerned, security—certainty—is the highest relative value. That which is most certain and secure is of most value and most highly reinforced by the ego, the self.

Therefore, we tend to form a psychological attachment to our status quo, and to resist serious indications of pending change. We are possessed by the "known," and disturbed by the unknown.

We desire to make the unknown known, to bring it into our realm of psychological control. Anything which is a threat to our knowledge of ourself, our existence, we make an effort to control. We *suppose* that we can exercise our will and can thus bring what *is*, into the state of what we believe, or feel, *should* be.

Our actions really are a series of reactions. All of these actions are based on motives; they have a goal, for which we're willing to make an effort in the expectation of gaining our reward. The "actions," prompted by our calculative mind, are *reactions* to the changes taking place around us.

The primary reaction is the establishment and maintenance of the self as an entity: self-separateness. Once the concept of psychological time has been rooted in the mind, and the sense of a separate self created (which exists in time), every other division-by-interpretation follows: *past* and *future* have been separated, drawn out, from *now*; I have a *self* which I believe exists independently of every *other* thing; I am *this* abstraction but I can become *that* abstraction; this development is *good* for my ego/security, that development is *bad* for my ego/security (or, succinctly, "me").

The psychological conflicts we face in life are the result of the divisions that we envisage: "they" (other imaginary selves) don't like "me" (an imaginary self).

These divisive abstractions do not exist independent of thought. Speculative thought is the activity of the ego, the self. The self does not exist except in relation to thoughts of past and future; there is no self in the present moment. There is no need to *become* in the present moment (or even "from moment to moment"); the moment, the "what is," is without effort.

But just as the moment is empty of all abstractions, the mind must be empty of the concept of self—to be in the moment where there is no division (and thus no conflict). When the mind is empty of the thoughts of self, there are no such drives (concepts, expressed through the emotions) as hope or despair. Therefore, there is no fear of not becoming, nor is there any ambition to become.

"Your" True Nature

If you go back to the earliest writings, the vedic Gitas and Upanishads, you notice how difficult it was to speak about enlightenment using words.

But over the centuries, the teachings have been refined and clarified. And they continue to become simpler to comprehend.

Even today, though, a seeker—I know from experience—reads many books, watches various videos, and listens to different speakers. Through that piecemeal process, we try to discover the meaning of the teachings. What I've found is that, in many cases, some element gets left out or overlooked.

The first thing I've noticed, is that people give little thought to some of the key words. The most obvious among these is a word which every spiritual tradition uses to describe the ultimate reality; omni-present.

This omnipresence is what is known as God or the Supreme Being, to some; Ramana Maharshi uses the word Self to describe it. In other words, it's not *apart* from the human self; but, at the same time, *more than*.

Whether we call it Omnipresence, God, or Self, it has crucial significance in how we understand "I," "you," and "world" or "reality": in other words, our life—and what is pertinent to it.

From the standpoint of a dualistic perspective, there is "I" and "others"; or, collectively, "us" and "them." The "others" and the "them" make up the "world" that "I" am in relationship with, my so-called relative "reality." It is in the context of *this* reality that our human suffering pertains. What is one to do about the suffering in the world, the exploitation, aggression, the turmoil?

The enlightened spiritual masters have said for millennia that the turmoil all begins with an "I"; that to be self-centered, self-interested, is basically a state of confusion, or "ignorance."

What is perceived as "my thoughts" orbit around an "individual"—separative—I. And we view these egoic thoughts as the guide for our behavior, for our every action. These "personal" thoughts are, in a word, self-serving; even the idea of "selflessness" can somehow become self-serving.

With the I-thought at the fulcrum of divisive and selfish behavior, these spiritual teachers advise us, we need to examine whether there is an alternative point of view which is more humane; *inclusive* of other "persons," rather than *exclusionary*.

This *spiritual* viewpoint, that is spoken of, is based upon a "realization of true nature" which has been intuited by perceptive people, irrespective of time or place. Its fundamental premise is that there is a universal or cosmic Presence which is free of any hinderance across time or space: infinite and eternal. As such, it is *a priori* the ground, or source, of being.

That is to say that every thing has been dependent upon this Presence; *existence* itself. Thus, as the so-called First Principle, *it* is the origination (or "creator") of our cosmos, earth, bodies, minds, thoughts, actions and their consequences; all that appears as *creation* as well as all that appears as *destruction*.

The sage views all that occurs as one unbroken movement; as a verb, be-*ing*. Celestial bodies, planets, animate and inanimate forms of life, conscious awareness, causes and their effects—this infinite and eternal *fundament* is responsible for every perplexing or paradoxical phenomenon we sense.

So this *insight*, said in the simplest way, is that every meaning that we give to something is reducible to the recognition that only one thing is ever happening: an expression of Be-ing. *Everything* is simply that one Truth. This is what is meant by "true nature."

Not everyone has come to realize true nature in a conscious way; this can be noticed, because such a realization obviates, or invalidates, the supposition that any "person" is the independent doer of the activities done; the originator of one's thoughts; or the controller of causes and effects. This lack of recognition of true nature applies to both the *individual* and the *collective*.

Therefore, coming to recognize the illusiveness of the I-thought has a relational influence on society from moment to moment. The point of the spiritual teachings is that there is no 'I' outside of, or beyond, or independent of the Self (or God, if you prefer). There are no thoughts or actions that are independent of the one omnipresent, *originating* Source. There are no activities of the world, creative or destructive, over which the individual or society has ultimate control. All of what appear to be isolated "effects" are the continuous consequence of the initiating, timeless Cause. This is what is meant by true nature.

So, an understanding of true nature will make it possible to understand what enlightened masters are saying when they speak of *non* duality, and its perspective on "you" and your "world" view.

The following statements of Ramana Maharshi will be clear, in this context:

> "All that is meant is that the Self is infinite, inclusive of all that you see. There is nothing beyond it, nor apart from it.... The source may be said to be God, or Self... If we first know the Self, then all other matters will be plain to us....
>
> "Intellect (thinking) is only an instrument of the Self.... There is only one Consciousness.... [Thoughts] arise from the Self....Mind (otherwise) does not exist.... The mind is only a projection from the Self. The Self continues to exist in the absence of the mind...(but mind) cannot exist apart from the Self.... 'Your' mind, and intellect (thoughts), are the factors of your wrong identity ('I').... Give up this mistaken identity, and... Self will be seen to be the single, nondual Reality.... For a realized being, the Self *alone* is the reality."

The true nature of the thinker of thoughts is the Self. The true nature of the doer of all deeds is likewise the Self. "Do not think that you are the doer.... (The actions) are not your own. They are God's activities.... Let us not pose as the doers."

To those who take the view of being somehow apart from, or independent of, the Self, "other individuals" will likewise be viewed as additional objects, to the object called "me." And as "me" and "others" are conceived to be separate objects, so too the "world" will be seen as yet an additional "part" of "objective reality."

What we suppose we see as an objective, or independent, world is essentially a separative or dualistic *thought*. Thoughts have their source in the Self. The conceived "individual" self is, in its true nature, the ever-present Self. When the 'I' comes to recognize its true nature, this Self-realized being then looks out upon "others" and the activities in the "world" and sees everywhere only its indivisible Self.

Ramana counsels:

> "You are not instructed to shut your eyes from the world. You are only to see your 'self' first, and then see the whole world as the Self."

Thus, for those who ask, "What is to be done about conditions in the world?," Ramana replies:

> "First set yourself right, and *then only* set out to improve 'others'. Change the *hearts* of men and the *world* will surely change. But one must begin somewhere; and one can begin only with oneself."

Are You Motiv-ated?

Buddha continually maintained that to end suffering, desire must come to an end.

The reason is that desire is a more readily noticed expression of one's often unacknowledged *discontent*.

We are so highly conditioned to accept that our constant judgments of the way things "should" be (or "could" be) are "normal", that we are often unaware of our chronic dissatisfaction with the way things actually *are*. But our desires—to turn our present condition into some alternate condition deemed more satisfactory—are generally more apparent in our conscious thought.

We are continually seeking after that which we don't have, rather than finding contentment in what is already present, the 'what is'.

So, desire is the symptom of our feverish condition of "becoming," most readily visible in our expressed desire of becoming "more happy"—satisfied—or "less unhappy."

Discontent is our harbinger of existential suffering. Desire is the reaction which is consciously noticeable, because it is the motivator for virtually all of our actions and activities.

In other words, each of our motivations, when considered, can alert us to the potential for an addition of impending suffering.

Today's Entree

It's a Chinese restaurant. The owner is from Korea. The waitress wears running shoes, black spandex ski pants, a frilly white blouse with a black bow tie. She is Mexican and speaks broken English.

The couple in the booth have ordered the Peking Palace Sunday-night Special, Egg Foo Yung. For appetizers, they have ordered martinis. The owner goes behind the bar, toward the back of the restaurant, and adjusts the sound on the color television mounted high in the corner of the room. From the fridge, he extracts a pair of chilled glasses; he pours into these a previously-mixed clear liquid, drops a pitted olive into these, and spears each one with a toothpick. The waitress is signaled to serve the cocktails.

Sipping their drink, the couple talks little. His face is baggy, like hers, and he has dark pouches under each eye. Over the front of her blouse hangs a maroon napkin, which she has tucked in under her collar.

He chews and swallows the olive, and begins to choke, making a great effort to appear not to be choking.

"Drink some water," she says.

He manages to gasp, "I don't know what I'd do if I didn't have you to tell me what to do!"

The Egg Foo Yung arrives. It is basically an omelet containing a few tired bean sprouts; it appears to have been deep-fried. It has been smothered in a stiff gravy which seems to have been designed to match the color of the omelet. Sprinkled atop this are a few green peas and diced carrots, who lived the greater part of their life in a can or a freezer.

When the waitress brings two small bowls of white rice, the omelet is already about to become history. "How is it?" she asks.

"Delicious!" the man booms. Looking at his wife, he says, "How come you can't cook like this?"

She is looking past him, watching television as she eats. A commercial exhibits a happy, energetic Oriental family who are gathered around a big table. They are delightedly eating a variety of glistening Chinese foods, while they jointly praise the wise old Chinese woman who proudly watches from the kitchen door. The camera closes in on her smiling face, and then zeroes in on the empty Chung King cans and packages on the kitchen counter behind her.

Alas, "life" is an empty façade.

Your True Identity

That which is purely the essence of all things is sometimes spoken of as "unitary consciousness," Mind, Brahman, cosmic intelligence, etc. And it is sometimes said that "out" of this essence, this one actuality, all other things are manifested.

But it must be clearly recognized that this essence is not something which has a center somewhere. And so, when it is said that plurality "manifests" from singularity, this is not to say that something is "coming out of" something else (as in childbirth). There is not a One standing apart in readiness to impart the Many.

The One is infinite, omnipresent: it has already always been all that is. And in its infinity, it is "outside" the pale of time; knowing nothing of duration or sequence—nay, only simultaneity—it is not the predecessor of any other thing. To *manifest* means to "make evident," to express, not to manufacture. And, in this case, that which expresses is itself expressed by the expression. That which is giving birth, to put it another way, is itself always at the same moment being born; neither womb nor fruit is more fundamental or preliminary than the other.

A nagging idea—which even the most ardent of the *religious* thinkers have difficulty surpassing—is that the Absolute "existed" before (and, in that way, apart from) us, and that out of this pre-existing condition we were "created" or "manifested."

Even if we were to take as a provisional premise that *essence* which is present in every iota of matter and energy, and at every point of form or void, it would form a singular, whole connection—the only denominator of all things. As the basic, common identity of all things—the Hindus would call this Brahman—if we were to ask what any particular "thing" *is*, primarily, we would have to answer that it is primarily Brahman. (Or whatever name we choose to give it.) Principally, we would have to say that—at the "bottom line"—it is the *only* thing which does actually *wholly* exist.

In other words, it can be said that essentially all things (the Many) *are* this essence (the One). That which truly *is*—whether we speak generally *or* specifically—is Essence.

That means that you are It, I am It, all things are It. Therefore, in this context, there is not any "thing" which is *apart from* any other "thing": all things are It.

And this is the point which many have failed to grasp. *Being all things*, it has no separate or particular identity *of its own*. It occupies no special place or center, it exists in no particular sequence or duration, it has nor holds not anything to itself. In short, it *has* no self. And in fact, in this sense, it can be said to be Void, Nothing or Empty (and, frequently, is said to be all of these).

When this aspect of the Absolute can be comprehended, a startling discovery can unfold. This, which has no identity of its own, in a peculiar way does *not exist*: this Absolute, in other words, has no choice but to eternally be unknown to "itself." Put another way, if all things are Brahman, there is not anything outside of that condition which can recognize that there *is* Brahman. Brahman, we could say, does not exist, unless some aspect or element of Braham manifests its existence.

Is that where *you* appear? Your capacity to recognize Intelligence *is* this Intelligence in re-cognition of itself. The Absolute, being all things (including *you*), anything which any aspect of it contemplates is It contemplating Itself. Put differently, it is only through your unitary consciousness that the One can *be* conscious: even when you are merely conscious of yourself, you are conscious of "more than" yourself. Though you may not be *aware* of it (although you *can* be), you are always supremely, wholly conscious. *You* are consciousness *itself*, to the extent that there is any consciousness in existence in the cosmos.

As Shankara says, It is not the "object" of anything "but its own self."

The Meaning of Love

Because it is so much at the very root of spirituality, an entire book could be written on how love is perceived by an enlightened being. As a pastor, you are asking how love is expressed in the context of nonduality.

By the way you framed the question, I think we can agree that we are not considering love in its common conception as mere affection and attachment toward another person or object; benevolent concern for other animate beings; romantic or sexual attraction; or worship and devotion toward an idol or supernatural image. All of these are relationships which reflect a dualistic perception. As Ramana Maharshi has said of this, "When you talk of 'love', there is duality, is there not: the person who loves and the entity...who is loved."

In the *transcendence* of the *dualistic* perception is the profound love which the nondual sages refer to. The Sanskrit term *ananda* is often translated into English as "bliss," but the bliss is the consequence of experiencing unconditional love: the word *unconditional* is defined as "absolute." This is love for all that exists: that means the "good," the "bad," and whatever is in between. It means a love that inclusively makes no distinction between what is manifested, from moment to moment, and the omnipresent Totality which manifests it.

Ramana uses various words to indicate the ever-present actuality, such as God or Self, that to which all things owe their be-ing. So he says, "expansion of love and affection would be a [proper] term for a true devotee of God," or the sublime Presence. But he emphasizes that this infinite Presence "is not 'somewhere else', but is inside [as well as outside] of each of us; so, in loving *all*, one loves only the *Self*.... The individual is not separate from God."

He is telling us that *this* love and affection expands to embrace the good, the bad and the indifferent—in *ourselves*, equally as in *others*. This is the "unconditional" aspect, which relates to our being nonjudgmental and non-interfering, and thus eliminates conflict, inward and outward.

This "love" is not an alternative to "hate"; it's the transcendence of divisive polarities: such as that some people, or developments, are "good" or "bad"; or that they *should* be this way, and *should not* be that way. This is what Ramana means by "the *absence* of love *or* hatred."

The infinite Being is above hatred, and above love as well, in the discriminating sense. But that, within each of us, which has the capacity for the expression of unconditional love, or compassion, is a manifestation of the Presence which loves itself through the medium of being all things which can be the subject of love.

Thus Ramana says:

> "Love is not *different* from the Self...[in this sense] God is love.... Love itself is the actual form of God.... Call it pure bliss, God, or what you will.

> "It is only through *jnana* [Self-realization] that the bliss that derives from true love will arise.... Die yourself [into the eternal Self] and lose yourself, becoming *one* with love.... To be the [nondual] Self, that you really are, is the only means to realize the bliss that is ever yours."

So, in summary: God *is* love (as well as all else), and this God manifests as *all* that is.

Let Go

Through our conscious experience, all of us have recognized that there are such physical actualities as "fullness" and "emptiness"; or, in abstract terms, form and void. Considering that everything which we experience has—to our mind—limits, is it so difficult for us to acknowledge the implication that something, "somewhere," has the possibility of existing without *any* limitation whatsoever? Can we concede that there is something which is not imprisoned even by man's arbitrary definitions of such realms as "space" and "time"? Can we conceive that there may be a void which is not defined by form; or a fullness that is found in emptiness? Can we understand that there must be—by implication—at least *one* thing in existence which does *not* make rational sense?

Once we loose the hobbles of our normally calculative thinking and we embrace the possibility that a reality exists that is entirely devoid of boundaries, we will perceive that this reality (of necessity) must be present in *every* place, at *all* times—in its *full* totality. In other words, there can be no place or time where it has not been, is not now, or will not be.

Since it has neither need to expand nor contract (considering that it has no requirement to "fit into" anything), it does not diminish or enlarge at any point where it is present—it is *complete* reality wherever it happens to be. Therefore, it does not reduce itself to fragments; there are no "parts" of a boundless reality: there is only reality, entirely manifest in all things.

Being fully present at each and every point and place, there is no place too large nor any point too small for its actuality. It is, for example, within every molecule, in every atom. And since it comprises everything, there can exist not even a border which is not itself composed of it. Therefore, being both fully "inside," fully "outside," and permeating anything "in between," it is not merely form *or* emptiness—it is *all* that there is. There can be, in reality, no tangible partition or barrier anywhere, between anything, since all things are of its composition.

It permeates the physical body, which subjective thought has defined as "you." It permeates that which you view as the interface of ("between") your form and that which you believe is "outside" of your body.

It is fully contained within you, at the very same moment that you are fully contained within it. You are not a "part" of it, nor is it a "part" of you. You are *it*, in the same way that it is *you*.

Being free of limitation and without a specific form, it is not static or fixed in its activity. It *is* what change *does*; it is in constant flux, in what we might term the process of creation and destruction. It is a "process," however, in which creation and destruction are *coincident*; this limitless energy knows nothing of beginnings, endings or temporal continuity.

Hence, the physical body which experiences creation also experiences destruction. Yet, the destruction of a physical body is not annihilation, it is transformation; though changed in form, no "part" of this energy disappears— for there is nowhere for it to relocate to where it is not already present.

From its conception, the physical body continually changes; as does the mind which "inhabits" it—as well as the "self" which occupies that mind. Upon death, change will continue in the form of the body, and of the mind, and of the self. The body is a physical reality, and its changes will be in the form of a material reality. The mind and the self are immaterial, and their changes will be in the nature of a formless reality.

We do not have control over reality; we cannot dissuade the energy of change. Death of the physical body is resolute; there has never been a mind that was without change; there is not a self whose constancy can be relied on. We can only attempt to temporarily avert or avoid that which we view as the impact of change. We can only attempt to control the workings of our mind, and attempt to improve the condition of our self. And there is no certainty of achievement, no assurance of security. There is but one certainty, and it is that the energy of change can destroy every of our efforts at control. Might we not, then, face this certainty by abandoning our efforts at control, attuning ourselves instead to the nature of change around and within us?

In the same way that we can, while alive, abandon our resistance to the death of the body, we can relinquish our resistance to the disappearance of subjective thought and of the personal self. That is, in the absence of making an effort to change our thinking and to change our selves, we can acknowledge observed changes without a decision to oppose, resist or assist them. We can silently concur in nature's transformations when and as they occur.

When we allow our subjective mind and our personal identity to drift away, where can our sense of personal presence go but to re-associate with that which is without boundary?

Wishful Thinking

There are those who believe that if they're not experiencing giddiness or euphoria, they could not be Self-realized. Their idea is that enlightenment ought to provide at least the thrill of a roller coaster ride, only just more persistently. *Ecstasy* is a product created in an illicit lab, it's not a reward for awakening from self-centeredness.

There is, indeed with Self-realization, a feeling of relief or release, a relaxation of tension, and a sense of peacefulness: because now there is no "self" to fret over, no "others" to chronically react to, nor even a "God" to be petulantly judged by. There is a placid state of contentment for which the word "bliss," misleadingly, comes nearest to describing.

This bliss is more accurately defined as *equilibrium*, a recognition that all things are equal in their sameness of ultimate, or absolute, nature. In the Sanskrit scriptures, the word is *ananda*, and it is clearly a consequence of Self-realization. The constant abiding in ananda is what is known as Sahaja Samadhi, the perception of "no self."

As Ramana states:

> "There is no difference between the enlightened and the unenlightened in their *conduct*: the difference lies only in their *perception*. The unenlightened identifies himself with the ego...whereas the ego of the enlightened has been lost...

> "To realize bliss, one realizes the Self.... Self-realization is bliss; it is realizing the Self as the limitless.... The ego is lost, and bliss remains.... Thus the Self is realized,

and bliss results.... Bliss consists in not forgetting your Being."

If an ecstatic state is what you are interpreting as ananda, Ramana adds,

> "...you feel great bliss and happiness and want to stay in that ecstasy. Do not yield to it, but pass on to the next stage which is great calm. The calm is higher than ecstasy and it merges into Samadhi."

In identifying with a self-affirming phenomenal sensation, there remains a subtle duality. But the source of the phenomena and the organism experiencing it are the same one, omnipresent Self. Ecstasy can become,

> "...an obstacle, because (in that state) a feeling of *separation* from the *source* of ananda, enabling the enjoyer to say '*I am enjoying ananda*', is present. Even this has to be surmounted. The final stage of Samadhi has to be reached in which one *becomes* ananda, or *one with reality*. In this state, the duality of enjoyer and enjoyment ceases in the ocean of sat-chit-ananda, or the Self.... *Be* the Self and *that* is bliss."

Get Serious

There is a type of spiritual seeker who can not be effectively aided.

He or she is looking for a quick and easy solution to life's quandaries—the least amount of investment or taxation, the better.

Any teacher is able to tell whether a person has done their homework or not. But there are, as in any endeavor, those who expect to get the benefit of the teaching while spending the least amount of time considering the subject matter.

Anyone who has anything to teach, prepared themselves to teach it. Their discoveries, in the subject, did not likely come without an expenditure of effort and resources. A student can benefit only by asking the right questions, informed questions, questions which have a well-grounded premise. "Tell me, in a few sentences, how to live in bliss"— or words to that effect—is not the kind of question which signifies that the questioner is prepared to seriously engage the instructions that will be given.

Your Essential Condition

Ramana's teaching was that the Self (Absolute) alone is. There is not anything which that is not, therefore it is in no way *apart* from anything. Though this is so, we do not automatically recognize that our fundamental condition is that we are in essence none other than That.

It is this Absolute of which "all that is," is manifest. Among the manifestations are the human organism, its brain, its sense organs, the thoughts which arise, the mind which is comprised of these thoughts, and the ego by which the organism declares "*I see.*"

It is this ego—self identification—which constructs the subject-object duality: me, and that which I do not perceive as me. Though this separative bias seemingly causes us to view the subject *I* as dissociated from anything which is not recognized as the body-brain-mind-ego, it is in fact nothing more than another manifested product of the omnipresent Self.

You—all elements and aspects of you, including the ego which posits otherwise—are only the Self. When this is clearly realized, it is realized that there *is* no individual ego (*all* egos, as is everything else, are the same Self), and the subject-object bias disintegrates. There is then recognized to be but one thing—the seer which sees no "other," separate object. This *Self*-realization has been the condition of the jnani throughout the ages, expressed at least 3,500 years ago as Tat Tvam Asi: That Thou Art. (*Whatever* "that" is.)

Ramana focuses on the self-awareness, which each seeker has, of his/her own existence. That very existence is essential to the Self. Our true nature, or identity, can be summarized as "I am." Anything which follows, or is added on to that, is merely another extension or elaboration of the Self: e.g., "I am the doer"; the *Self* is the doer. "I am the thinker"; the *Self* is the thinker.

Ramana utilized particular ways in which to attempt to bring the seeker to recognize his/her underlying essence. (And on some rare occasions, the seed of realization was obviously planted, as evidenced by the listener confirming having gotten the point.)

For example, in our relative, human condition, it could be said that there are three different but connected levels of consciousness: what we consider to be our "normal" condition, when our eyes are open and we are wide awake and in relationship to the "real world"; when our eyes are closed and our body in repose, yet the thinking, imaginative mind is still functioning in support of our discriminating ego, and we are acting in relationship to an acknowledged unreal "dream world"; and when consciousness has sunk beneath the stage of thought and ego identification, and we are in a deep, death-like, "unconscious" condition, dream-free and thought-free. The connecting thread in all of these varied, cyclical conditions is consciousness; if consciousness ceased to be present in any of these three conditions, the life cycle would end.

While consciousness is the underlying and connecting presence in all three conditions, it varies in its manifest form in each. In the awake state, it is the substratum on which the ego interacts with material elements and phenomenon considered to exist objectively in time and space. In the dreaming phase, it is the screen upon which the mind plays images and possibilities, free of the constraints of limiting time, space or cause-and-effect. In the period of deep sleep, consciousness exists free of the imposition of cognitive thought and interpreted sense impressions; pure empty awareness with no "real" or "unreal" object envisioned. This aspect of unadulterated, unconditioned consciousness is our absolute essence, the common and unitary presence at the core of each and *every one* of us.

Since this indiscriminate presence is our fundament at every moment, it is permanent and unchanging. It is our true Self, upon which our changing self—and its consequent thoughts, emotions, actions, etc.—are passing, inconsequent phenomena.

In deep sleep, we neither affirm nor deny our existence; we simply are—as (and what) we are—without any identification or I-centeredness and also without any idea of objective phenomenon, either "real" or "unreal." The "world"—and every "other" thing—is nonexistent in this presence. When we recognize our essence (in our waking state), the false identification as a separate I dissolves. This is Self-realization, plain and simple.

In All Humility

There is a houseplant on the patio table. For a few weeks before, it had been on the nightstand near my bed. It has no choice as to where it resides.

If it is left in a dark room for too long, it will weaken and succumb. If it is left for too long in the full sun, its leaves will sunburn and fall away. It depends upon me to water it regularly, or it will wilt and die.

Wherever it happens to be, and whatever the circumstances of the care or lack of care it's given, it does at all times only what it *can* do. To the extent that it survives, it flourishes; to the extent that it languishes, it dies. It goes from moment to moment responding to the present situation entirely and exactly as is—without any resistance whatsoever.

Composed of the same living energy that I am, wherever it goes when it dies is where I go. Whatever the meaning of its life while it lives is the meaning of my life. Whatever the nature of its connection in the wholeness, so is my connection.

Be, or Not to Be?

What did Ramana say about *sadhana* ("path"); that is, "practice" such as meditation? "People seem to think that by practicing some elaborate sadhana, the Self would one day descend upon them.... Sadhana implies an object to be *gained*, and the means of *gaining* it.... *I* had no rules of meditation or contemplation. Meditation is possible only if the ego be kept up."

In other words, the aspirants' idea is that "if I do some procedure, process or ritual correctly, and if I do it long enough, I will come in contact with ultimate Reality": it will someday "descend upon them."

The irony is that the presence of ultimate Reality—ever-present everywhere at all times—not only surrounds the meditator (whether or not meditating), and in fact imbues—is the very essence of—every meditator or non-meditator. There is nowhere you can go, and nothing you can do, that can ever bring you "closer" to That (or Self) than you are in any moment.

This is precisely why the teachings say "there is nothing to *get*; you *are* what you are seeking!" The seeker supposes herself to be some thing other than That, and That to be the *object* which one will encounter. This is what in Buddhism, is called a "gaining idea": *I*, subject, will somehow *gain* (or come into possession of) *It* (or knowledge of It: "enlightenment"), the object of my pursuit in time.

The subject, supposing that she's separate from the Self she seeks, is still regarding herself as an "individual," an independent entity. This *person-al* identification is what Ramana is referring to as the ego. Only as long as this *individual* identification is maintained can the self *not* be realized to be the Self she would propose to "encounter." All she would need to do is, one time, get to the bottom of the query Ramana phrases as "who (or what) *am* 'I'?" The *seers'* answer is, That, the Self.

Were the meditator to recognize that all activity (such as meditating, or not meditating) is an inadvertent expression of the omnipresent Self, she would comprehend that the "two"—the Self, and all activity which is a manifest expression of it—are merely aspects of the same singular actuality. The pointlessness of meditating as a *means* to an *end* is as apparent as this: any activity that is reflected in a mirror (by "individuals") is not independent of the mirror (ultimate Reality). To presume that the meditator could somehow ever be apart from ultimate Reality is obviously a dualistic distinction which leads *away* from the recognition of "oneness."

> "...Realize the pure, *undifferentiated* being of the Self, or Absolute....
>
> "'Intentional' meditation involves a subject who has some objective.... You must learn to realize all 'subject' and 'object' as *one*; and in the *meditating*, you are destroying that sense of oneness—and creating duality....When the sense of separateness is lost, and the *objective* of meditation along with the *subject* who meditates is left behind—without anything else to know—it is Realization.... The Realized has *become* the Self, and there is nothing more to do.... *This* is enlightenment."

When the seeking thus ends, the seeker has understood that there is not anything she needs to do, or practice, in order to *be* the Self which has (amusingly) been sought. To be as you *are* is to be the Self! One's *self*-identity is recognized as the *Self's* identity: undifferentiated.

> "No aids are needed to know one's own Self; that is, to be aware.... Liberation is only to *remain* aware of the Self. No long process is necessary to know the Self.... I am saying that the Self is self-evident.... Why do you wish to meditate at all?... Why do you not remain as you are without meditating?... Self is realized not by one's doing something, but by one's *refraining* from doing anything; by remaining still and *being* simply what one really *is*."

To simply "remain aware of the Self" is what "meditation" *truly* means to the Self-realized. It is an effortless, unconstrained perception of ultimate Reality which is the "present awareness," whether one is active or inactive, throughout the waking hours. It is not a matter of attempting to control one's thoughts or restrict one's attention: no matter what is thought, said or done, it is regarded as the doing of the Self, or ultimate Reality. *Whatever* is observed—positive or negative or neutral—"that *too* is It!" This frees one from such (dualistic) concerns as "am I being *aware*? Or was I momentarily focused on some activity and was temporarily *un*aware?"

> "When thoughts cross the mind and an effort is made to neutralize them, the effort is usually termed 'meditation'.... Remain as you *are*. *That* is the aim.... To make the mind 'subside'...the mind will remain in an apparent state of subsidence, but will rise again.... What does it matter if the mind is active? It is so only (as) the Self!... Why do you worry 'I didn't' [or 'I did']

meditate?... If the idea 'I did' or 'I didn't' is given up, all actions will end up as meditation.... This, indeed, is the state called sahaja samadhi.... Then 'meditation' cannot be given up. Even if we 'give it up,' it will not let go of us. This is sahaja samadhi [full awakening]."

In the first work he ever wrote (c. 1901, at 22), paradoxically 'practice' amounted to freedom *from* practice. To remain as you are, while realizing *who* you are, is to *practice* being a perfect expression of the Self.

"This is Liberation: never to be heedless of one's own *all perfect* pure Self is the *acme* of...forms of spiritual practice."

Reply to Sharon

Yes, my monograph was rather abstract; an *example* of what is meant *would* help.

At the Zen farming commune (Big River Farm), we had no regular, on-site teacher. A deep and persistent reading of Suzuki Roshi's *Zen Mind, Beginner's Mind* was our main source of instruction. Some of us began to walk like and quack like Suzuki Roshi.

I was strolling in the forest ("in the stillness") one afternoon, with nothing in particular on my mind. Two words came to me, as if they had been spoken ("as if the universe were summoning attention"): BE YOURSELF.

I recognized immediately what that meant: rather than attempting to be an imitation Suzuki Roshi, the spiritual teachings are urging me to be the genuine Self. Suzuki Roshi was an expression of the Self; Robert Wolfe is to be an expression of the Self, not an expression of some idealized—and idolized—Zen master.

(So, an "insight received that transformed consciousness." Less abstract?)

By Any Other Name

Ramana uses the attribution "Self" in the same way that other teachers use the word Absolute. He wants you to understand that your *true* "self" is not different than the Self.

But the true self which Ramana points to, your Absolute self, has no characteristics. You might conclude that you are insufficient in this quality or that quality, but your Absolute nature is beyond the limitations of any quality. Qualities—pro or con—are a concoction of your mind.

In other words, your beingness as Self is not dependent upon whether you are adjudged to be an adequate person or an inadequate person. A rose with five petals is not less of a rose than one with twenty-four petals. The Self is all that is, as Ramana says. The Self, then, constitutes the inadequate as well as the adequate.

*

No sky...
No earth...
But still,
Snowflakes fall!
– Kajiwara Hashin

The Sacred

Nancy:

Combining some of your queries.

When Nisargadatta (or Ramana) says Self (with a capital S), he means the same as the Absolute, Brahman, God, or any other name for the infinite and eternal formless Reality.

Being without limited form of its own, it is said to be ubiquitous, omnipresent. As such, it permeates, saturates all that has apparent form (such as human bodies). That is *why* the teachers say "you are That," or "God and you are in no way separate," etc.

So, N. is saying (first) that the Self cannot "exist" without there being some thing which recognizes, acknowledges, "knows" that it does indeed have reality. This is where *you* come in: operating "through" you—*as* you—It has the potential to recognize its Self. When you wake up to the fact that your "true nature" is the Absolute, It (as "you") is now self-aware (Self-aware). Thus, N. says, "The Self cannot experience its knowingness [Self/self-awareness] without the help of the body."

Secondly, this is only *comprehended* when you finally get the point that *there are no two things*.

The Absolute is not a separate entity, in any way *apart* from the body (which you think of as "you"). It appears to you that the Absolute is "invisible," and you are visible. But the Absolute is the essence, the *"true* nature" of every *visible* speck of matter (and every invisible atom which composes that matter) that it is possible for you to see.

The Vedas say, "not two; not one." There are not *two* things—separate entities—"me" and "It," regardless of the fact that this may *seem* to be what's apparent (in its visible form) to you.

And: there is not *one* thing, in the sense that anything is an isolated, independent object; *every* "thing" is, at its common denominator, That. And even That is not a "thing," an entity, being entirely without any form of its own.

Next. That is *why* N. says "I Amness [another name for Self (Absolute)] has no authority of its *own*." It is not some bearded old man, throwing down thunderbolts. It is *you*, and every thing that you think of as not-you. Whatever *It* does, it does *as* its myriad manifestations; therefore it is not something *apart*, wielding "authority." It need *have* no authority, because there is not one thing that could ever be in *opposition* to it, since it is already all (so-called) things.

Last. Any "image" is a representation of some "thing," such as any (so-called) thing that is reflected in a mirror. The Absolute is not a thing (separate entity), therefore—as you surmise—any image of it (such as Jehovah, Krishna, etc.) must be false. As you suggested, there could not be an image of that which is without any *form*. The word *idol* translates in Latin as "an image, or form"; its dictionary meaning is: "a representation of a god, used as an object in religious worship." To "idolize" anything is to "miss the mark."

Krishnamurti said that if you put a stone on the mantelpiece, and put flowers and a candle in front of it, before long people will be bowing to it. Since the Absolute is ("in") all things, no object is any more sacred or holy than any other.

A Nonprofit Venture

Sunny day. Light breeze. Afternoon walk. Residential neighborhood. A card table ahead, at the edge of a lawn.

Two girls on alert, tending to business. Asian. Straight black hair. Both wearing glasses.

The posterboard sign, taped to the table's front, printed by felt-tip pen:

ICECOLD LEMONAID ~~50 Cents~~ 25 Cents
COOKIES 25 Cents & 50 Cents

I'm considering the two types of cookies. The older girl points them out in turn: "Ginger snaps. From a box. Twenty five cents. They're small. Two would be fifty cents. The big ones are oatmeal raisin. We made them. They're just fifty cents." She entices me: "Those are my favorite."

I follow her recommendation, and find among my pocket change two quarters. She drops them in her open cash box. I may be the only patron at the moment, but a few dollar bills show that I haven't been the only customer all day.

The younger partner takes a small paper cup off of a stack and hands it to the co-owner, who raises a porcelain pitcher with both hands. "The lemons are organic. We grow them."

I nod, and she fills the cup. I sip with one hand, and search my change pocket again.

"This isn't ice cold lemonade," I report. "This is warm lemonade."

"Yes," says the older girl. "Technical difficulties."

"Actually," adds the younger, as if taking responsibility, "poor planning."

"So," says the older, with resignation, "we lowered the price."

I hand over my quarter. I ask, "What are you going to do with your profits?"

"It goes to our piano teacher," says the older.

"Piano lessons?"

The younger explains, "He has cancer."

I locate a dollar and place it in the paper cup labeled TIPS. "I suppose I can take a tax write-off," I muse aloud.

The two girls look at each other, quizzically.

"Dad will know," the younger says to the other assuringly.

The Impermanent I

Scientific research has revealed that we each have several periods of dreaming while we slumber each night. Interspersed, we also have periods of a deeper state of sleep in which dreams are absent. In this condition, were it not for the autonomic and metabolic systems which direct such functions as heartbeat, respiration, etc., our unconscious state would simply be a coma resulting in death.

However much our organism requires this period of comatose deep sleep daily, the body could not survive an endless interim of it; we need, at the very least, to actively feed ourself, replenish and expel liquids, employ the muscles, and so on.

From this mindless, unconscious condition of deep sleep, our cognitive "thinking mind" arises, expressing itself consciously in the figurative activity of a *dreaming* episode.

Once the cognitive process arises and *stabilizes* itself, wakened consciousness presides. We attend to our quotidian duties required for the organism's survival; retire nightly for rest from our wakened excursions; relax the cognitive consciousness into a state of its inactivity; and the inert deep sleep condition prevails as the normative state again.

The significance of this process (of the sleep cycle) is threefold: that of the *un-consciousness*; the pre-wakened *consciousness*; and then wakened, *active* consciousness. Identification of (or with) the organism as "myself" is only a phenomenon of the latter *two* categories.

Anyone whose sleep has been unbroken for a matter of several hours has experienced self-identification, or self awareness, present in a portion of that period, as recognized in *dreaming*. But for some period of time, unaccounted for by dreaming, there was an un-conscious, mind-less interlude: it was a state of being that was *absent* of self-identification.

While, as previously stated, a body cannot survive an indefinite period of un-conscious, comatose inactivity, it becomes clear that the organism can continue to function, hour by hour, *without* cognitive self-identification.

And, because there are no conscious conceptions or images in *deep sleep*, there is also no possibility for illusions. By contrast, in the *dreaming* state there are appearances and images which are entirely fantasy and illusion.

In the dreaming state, there is *self*-identification with the central dream figure, or at least the implied perceiver of the dream experiences. What is perceived by this dream "self" are objects, forms or images which are not—that is, are *other* than—this imagined, self identified, "person."

In the *deep sleep* state, there are no images, or even illusions, which occur in mind-less consciousness; there is not even a conception of 'I' as a "person," or even as a dream figure. As an agent to direct the activities of the body, such a self-identified entity is unneeded, since the autonomic and metabolic systems are in direct control.

The self-designation, as 'I', only begins to formulate in the *dreaming* "mind" as the cognitive process emerges in preparation for the wakened state. It is a fantasy entity which directs, or appears to react to, the projections in the dream.

Once the cognitive, "thinking" mind has stabilized itself by enacting the illusive developments in a dream, the subjective perceiver of the dream state (the person self-identified as 'I') begins to merge into the *awakened*, active state. During the awake period, the 'I' serves its role of directing activities as the agent, or "self," of the "person" who was conceived in the dreaming state.

Once the relative and necessary activities of our waking day are completed, we rest the body; the I-identification reverts to identification with a fantasy dream figure; and dis-appears entirely upon the onset of re-emergent deep sleep.

The 'I', or self identification, is a *temporary* super-imposition for functional relationship, both in the precognitive dream state *and* the wakened, cognitive and active, state. It originates, each day, out of a pre-awakening *illusory* condition, and dissolves each night back into an illusory condition.

We have no *control* over the arising or the disappearance of this temporary agency, or phantasm. Its purpose is to permit us to relate to and manipulate the material world, for the physical survival of the organism.

That it is not a necessary fixture during hours of our life is instructive: there is no substantive or sustained 'I' which is any more our *fundamental* identity than is empty presence which exists in the portion of our life that is free of "self" interest; dream-less sleep.

In other words, that "you" are *not* is at least as real as that you *are*.

*

"You experience the world due to your waking and sleep states. When you know the 'why and how' of these states, it is an end of all your search for knowledge."

– Nisargadatta

Revelatory Revolution

You're correct, of course, that whatever one's state of awareness, we have to each of us provide food and shelter for the body. And how we attend to this is what has been called "right livelihood"—in a relative world where circumstances are not ideal.

A suggested first consideration: to the extent that one is in confusion, all that one does is an acting-out of that confusion; to the extent that one has clarity, all that one does is an activity of that clarity. So the first item on the agenda needs to be this matter of arriving at clarity concerning the ultimate nature of our reality. When you know who, or what, is the true Doer of what's being done, this is the "right" foundation for subsequent "livelihood."

Then this consideration: ask not what you can get; ask what you can give. The lives of the enlightened masters tell us that when your wants and your needs are not two, you are likely to lead a non-competitive life, involving a freedom out of which emerges a fearless creativity; this becomes, without intention, a life of "service." And, like water reaching its own level, such service tends to be materially supported, without even the need to ask.

You write, "There is no *me*." Then allow the Doer to do what needs to be done, while living in that clarity.

Half Way Up

A journal (*The Link*), circulated among those who have been influenced by Krishnamurti, contained this (unsigned) account, abridged here:

"It was clear to the intellect, that it had to surrender…a state not unlike total abandonment…every inner movement came to an end…. I no longer felt any sense of separation…at the same time, it was completely normal…everything was wonderfully harmonized, and daringly simple and transparent. A new dimension was making itself manifest…it was an ecstasy of clarity, a plunging into the essence of things, into the plain straightforwardness of truth…

"This transformation came as a total surprise; I hadn't planned it…. The uncommon—where there is no longer any conflict of the opposites—became the companion of my days…that singular sense of *being* surfaced, at its strongest in quiet moments—when it also demanded the most attention, and revealed its fathomless profundity…. One was living (it seems to me), to the thousandth of a second, exactly in the present moment…as if all the screws, angle-irons and nails—which would normally hold the I-thought together—had simply fallen away…total insecurity and absolute security—that is, emptiness and fullness—were one and the same…which, naturally, goes beyond logic and normal understanding…not to revert to the power-seeking, or routine-type activities of the mind—but to be single and free of the chains of the past, and one with the Immensity of the moving present."

This certainly sounds like what might be called the "typical enlightenment experience." However, what follows does not sound *atypical* either.

> "...over the years, this revelatory experience has disappeared completely, into the unconscious... conventional life took over...the pressure toward fanciful projection (on which the world, and one's own brain, are built) could no longer be diverted... the (nosy) intellect gave its assent, with three cheers— saying how good it was to be snuggled up again in a *mediocre*, narrow, straight life...the old...triumphed again over the new...some ten years later, I am writing this report."

Enlightenment is not merely a wholly different way of *seeing*, Krishnamurti might have said, but a *wholly different* way of *living*.

It was after Krishnamurti's realization (a new way of *seeing*) that he took the action of dissolving the Order of the Star, and embarked on a freshly new way of *living*—rather than snuggling up again in a mediocre life. And for him this revelatory experience did not disappear under the pressures of conventional life, which he had forsaken.

Krishnamurti sometimes pointed out that mediocre means "half way up the mountain."

Wholly

The dualistic perspective is at the root of our fragmented lives. We perceive that we have a family life, a work life, a spiritual life, and so on, moving our attention in the weekly hours from one compartment to another.

We view the people we interact with as American or foreign, white or non-white, straight or gay, and distinctions more petty still.

And we live out a daily chain of reactions, attempting to indulge those things we like, and evade the developments we dislike.

As long as one lacks the wholistic view, the smooth completion that is embodied in the hub is lost to the blurring of the frenzied spokes.

Every line we draw becomes a limitation, a subliminal barrier. Every circle drawn around ourself shuts "me" in, and defends against the potential flow.

See that the entirety of life—and death—is a singular unbroken movement which isn't affixed to anything on either end. Not any distinction that we make is any more important than any other.

One Unbroken Movement

Comprehend that you are still living with a pre-Copernicus mindset.

A clergyman in a cathedral in 1543, Copernicus published a treatise postulating that the sun does *not* appear to rise and set as a consequence of it revolving around the earth (the latter of which the Church presumed to be the center of the universe). To the contrary, he asserted, the earth revolves around the sun, which is stationary; and it is the earth's axial rotation which provides the appearance of a rising and setting sun.

Nearly ninety years passed before *Galileo's* interest in physics and telescopes resulted in publication (in 1632) of experimental verification of Copernicus' revelation (followed by Galileo's trial before Rome's inquisition the following year).

Like the pre-Copernicans who were without doubt that the earth graced the hub of the universe, most people today still suppose that "cause and effect" is such a truism that it is an undeniable fact.

This was disproved, now more than 40 years ago!

Most people today would recognize the name of Alexander Graham Bell of the telephone, but not the name of Irish physicist John Stewart Bell. But the latter, in 1964, did for physics as much as Copernicus did for astronomy. And, as recently as 2004, Swiss physicist Nicholas Gisin established the revelation of Bell, as firmly as did Galileo that of Copernicus.

In sum, to quote physicist Nick Herbert:

"Bell's Theorem [a theorem is not a theory; it's been experimentally *proven*] states, in effect, that after two [subatomic] particles interact in a conventional way, then move apart outside the range of the interaction, the particles continue to influence each other *instantaneously* via a real connection, which joins them together with undiminished strength no matter how far apart they may roam....Bell's Theorem says not merely that superluminal connections are *possible*, but that they are *necessary* to make our kind of universe work....Bell's Theorem shows that... things are hooked together by an invisible, underlying network of superluminal connections."

Physics professor Lee Smolin:

"This means that the entangled nature of the quantum state reflects something *essential* in the world.... This makes it one of those rare cases in which an experiment [such as Gisin demonstrated over 31 miles, likened—given the relative size of particles—to 31 light-years across space] can be interpreted as a test of a philosophical principal [viz. nonduality]....We— who live in the universe, and aspire to understand it—are then inextricably part of the *same* entangled system."

Physicist Shimon Malin:

"Such a connection takes place because both events [the cosmic interaction by two—or more—particles] form a *single* creative act, a single '*actual entity*,' arising out of a common field of potentialities."

And physicist Henry Stapp:

"The important thing about Bell's Theorem is that it puts the dilemma posed by quantum phenomena *clearly* into the realm of *macroscopic* ["visible"] phenomena...(showing) that our ordinary ideas about the world are somehow profoundly deficient *even* at the macroscopic level."

Gary Zukov:

"Bell's Theorem tells us that there is no such thing as 'separate parts'. All of the 'parts' of the universe are connected in an intimate and immediate way... 'Commonsense' ideas are inadequate even to describe macroscopic *events*—events of the *everyday* world!" [e.g., cause and effect]

Renowned physicist David Bohm:

"We can say that *inseparable* quantum *interconnectedness* of the whole universe is the *fundamental* reality...any attempt to assert the *independent* existence of a 'part' would deny this unbroken wholeness... This form of description cannot be closed on the large scale, any more than on the small scale....This means that our *notions* of space and time will have to *change* in a fundamental way....The notion of the constitution of the world out of separately-existent parts is turned upside down....There are *indivisible* links of action between each object, and its environment."

This, then, is the physical *reality*, the actual *fact* of the universe that *we* live in.

There is no such *actuality*—throughout time and space, as we know it—as cause that is apart from effect.

Most people today are basing their assumptions on pre-Bell doctrine; just as most people, before 1543, based their assumptions on pre-Copernicus doctrine.

But in terms of how you live your life, based on the assumptions you are making, the former is more important than the latter.

Will ninety years pass before you incorporate the supportive scientific evidence of what the sages have maintained for some 3,500 years: "You are not the doer"?

A Primitive Concept

You're right, you won't generally see me using the word "soul." It is a hazy and archaic religious notion which supposes that "spirit" comes into the material body at some point in time, and exits at a subsequent time. The spirit or soul, of course, is claimed to be the "divine" part of a human being.

A Professor of Religious Studies has pointed out: "Roman Catholicism contends that the soul is created at conception; some Protestant groups have said it starts fourteen days after conception; a Jewish tradition says forty days after conception for boys and ninety days after for girls; and Islam maintains that an angel breathes the life force into the fetus 120 days into pregnancy. Though they disagree on the exact moment of 'ensoulment', the Western traditions are united in saying the soul comes into being at a particular moment in time."

Where, apart, is this soul lingering until an embryo begins to form? If, in time, it comes from somewhere and later goes somewhere, it is time-bound, temporal. It would be (at best) an object in movement within that which is eternal and unmoving—no different than the human body, which is transitory. Therefore, the soul itself is not the essence of being, which the divine ever-present is considered to be: it is of no more importance, compared to the ultimate reality, than is the impermanent body itself.

St. Denis, Bishop of Paris circa 250 A.D.: "The ultimate Reality is not soul...nor is it a spirit...."

Advaita Condensed

Both religious and spiritual teachers refer to the ultimate actuality as "omnipresent." When we use the word "present," we mean to indicate simultaneously "in present *time*" and "in present *place*"; that which is *present* is "here, now."

That is why the word "Absolute" is used universally as a name for the ultimate actuality: it is absolutely in *every* place at *all* times; as has been said "nowhere is It not." That is what omnipresent means: that which cannot *not* be existent in *every* possible place, at *any* conceivable time: it is *limit-less*.

Because the presence of the ultimate actuality is not confined to any *particular* place, the concept of "place" (as a significant point or area) has no meaningful *relevance* to the Absolute. And because the Absolute transcends all demarcations (concepts, really) of time, likewise *time* is *meaningless* in the context of omnipresence.

That is why, speaking from the standpoint of ultimate awareness, the sages collectively say, "Neither time *nor* space are reality." Both time and space are *relative*: relational, in terms of measure. (Measure is an arbitrary thought process.)

Since the omnipresent is found in *every* place-point, at *any* given time, it necessarily *permeates* all that is. Since you are among the "things" that *are*, you are not impermeable to the limitless all-present Absolute. Thus, the sages say: *That* you are.

That is the substance of (self) "realization."

Great Expectations?

"Contemplation of my real nature has certainly taken hold," you write. "Yet my life does not look much different, and habitual reactions are still appearing."

As a consequence of what one can find in much of the spiritual material, there is sometimes an exaggerated expectation as to how life will "look" after Self-realization.

Twenty, thirty, forty or more years of (dualistic) societal conditioning does not necessarily disappear overnight. There are some acquired habits, especially, which may not be amenable to much change at all.

The significant change that does relate to Self-realization is the relinquishing of the tendency to hope that the real facts of life will be something other than what they resolutely are.

For those who are viewing life from a *dualistic* framework, there will be an effort to move away from what is perceived as negative (or un-pleasant) and to move toward the positive end of the spectrum (whatever is deemed pleasant). The teachings of *nonduality* assure us that it is possible to transcend such dualistic distinctions, in our general perception, as "better" or "worse." In other words, we view matters in terms of 'what *is*,' rather than how they *could* be or *should* be.

Therefore, in the wake of Self-realization, the *world* (good, bad or middling) has not changed; but one's *perspective*, concerning all that one is aware of, has changed. Put another way, the world looks no different than it ever has— but our expectation, that it ought to appear any way other than it does, is recognized to be at the root of suffering and conflict.

So, we're not talking about the elimination of worldly reality, but of accordance with all of actuality; not exclusion, but inclusion.

This would be expressed by the nondual rishis as "Being present with what's *present*"—as contrasted to what one wishes or hopes was instead present.

As to "the dissolution of the ego," the "ego" is one of the dualistic ideas we have been enculturated to conceive as having substance. (Try to find an "ego" before Freud was born.) Is there an ego apart from an I? Ramana would put it this way: The ego is as real as the self. If there is no such separate entity as a "self," what becomes of the ego?

The notion of an "ego" is the scapegoat for a person's (mainly "undesirable") behavior. What role can an "ego" play for a person who no longer critiques her behavior in terms of "better" or "worse"? When you recognize your behavioral expressions to be 'what is'—factual in occurrence, rather than some would-be ideal—you will experience them as you would experience any other element of the 'what is.' This, then, is effectually the *dissolution* of the ego.

The fundamental question is, what is your "real nature"? If you say you "reject the conventional view of the separation of objects," is there a "you," a "self," that is in actuality apart from all else that is? If you comprehend that ultimately "everything is the Absolute," is there an "I" which is separate from *anything*?

How It's Known

No matter where you go in the cosmos—whether interstellar *space* or in contact with stellar *material*—an unbroken presence is there, a presence which is universal. It is *be-ing*, and it is never discontinuous with any moment in time.

This presence, or be-ing, is not confined within the universe, rather the universe exists *within* this condition of *present being.*

This be-ing is not restricted to externals; there is (this thing we call) presence on the *inside* of any material object, exactly as we say there is presence that is in *contact* with every object.

It is presence of this be-ing which informs every thing as to what is each thing's nature; that is, in what way its existence is to *be.*

No object or space is either too vast or too minute for be-ing to be present, around *or* within it.

We can say that all objects can be broken down into constituents. We can conversely say that all objects can be built up from such constituents.

So, objects are simply their components; and these components are merely the formative material of objects. Even empty space is infused with various existent components.

Be-ing is present in the grandest *objects*, existing as it does in the most finite of *components*.

It is this beingness which informs the *components* of the nature of the existence of each; and, in doing so, informs every *object* as well.

But while the finite components and the spatial objects are limited to the particular time and place in which each occurs, the presence of the universal beingness is not limited.

The components, or objects, are limited to the nature of their existence to which each has been informed; the present be-ing, which universally informs, is not limited by any particulars of time and place. It is what co-ordinates the interaction of all constituents with objects; and objects within their space and moment.

The present beingness does not *arrive* at, or in, the objects or constituents, in order to inform each of its nature, *meeting* them in some spatial time. The presence of beingness is the *locus* in which the finite has the capability to exist. Thus, it does not *enter* each object from an exterior; the object's *interior* can only *exist* in be-ing. So, beingness informs all universally, by being present in *and* around all, at every place and time.

Objects and constituents may be composed, and may be decomposed; but the present be-ing in which they exist (or cease to exist) remains unchanged and unmoving: it is universally existent everywhere, always.

Your body is a material object, composed of constituents limited in time and space. These constituents exist in a field of present beingness that coordinates, or governs, the disposition of the finite.

It does not coordinate these changes (in the forms) from *without*, but from *within*; that is, as if it *were* the forms, but without abrogating its universality concurrently.

In *being* all, it is *informing* all, and thus all is done in concordant harmony. Creation is dependent upon destruction, and destruction precipitates creation; and beingness is present in every such circumstance.

This beingness was present in the constituents which began to form your body. It governs every process of the body in time and space; the material processes (such as the construction of the brain), and the immaterial processes (such as thoughts and movements) which are a consequence of the material processes.

And the same beingness is no less present in the deconstruction, or deterioration, of your body and the consequent cessation of the immaterial processes.

When the body deteriorates, and decomposes, the constituents act on instructions to change their material composition, composing alternative forms. The beingness continues to be present, in that locus of time and space, because it is always already ever-present at every point of time and space.

In other words, this beingness did not *come to*, or *come into*, your body at some unique time and in some particular place. The constituents of your body have never been apart from present being; and your formed body has never operated, or acted, outside of the field of present being.

When your body disintegrates, the present being it has exited *in*, and *as*, does not disappear or relocate to some other place or time, as there is no other place or time where it is not already being present.

Every material form, and even spatial form, shares its existence with the same, singular field of present being. Knowing all forms, even from within, this beingness instructs the material (and immaterial) changes, movements, and actions. It is never, in any way, isolated from anything which is presently being.

The *forms* continually and constantly change. What *animates* the forms maintains itself as unchanged and unchanging—never *not* being present.

This is not *a* being, as if more than one such condition could be present universally. Nor is it conscious, though present as the condition which consciousness exists in; it is what informs the changes and movements of consciousness— making *being* conscious possible.

So, it is not *consciousness* which survives the deconstruction of any body, but the present beingness (which makes forms and their attributes possible).

What survives the body is not even "your" beingness, but *all* of beingness. Beingness was the presence in which your body formed, so it was not *added* to your form; it was already present in, and as, the formation.

And so, beingness is not subtracted from the body, as if it made a movement to some place, or time, where it was not already present.

We could say that consciousness *was* added to the form, inasmuch as consciousness is a by-product of the form, an immaterial process consequent upon the material.

Consciousness, then dissolves, with the form, into the universally present being.

Beingness was present in the formation of your body; beingness will be present in the dissolution of your body. In its universal presence, be-ing (itself) does not move or change; it is the condition in which movements and change are existent. It is the condition in which your bodily form is composed and dispersed.

At no time, or place, are you ever apart from this process. The constituents of your body will re-form into another form. All that will be left of you is the condition *in* which you were formed, and *into* which you dissipated: that is, the universal presence of be-ing, *in which* time and space exist, and which is already everywhere this very moment.

So, the "what you are" is *here*; has been here; and will be here—*regardless* of the presence of your body.

self to Self

Thanks for your letter. I can see that you were contemplating it, as you composed it line by line.

In nine vertical inches of type, the word "I" appears 34 times, "me" or "my" another 15 times.

At this point, you might find it useful to notice the arising of the I-thought (or me, my, mine etc.) on the screen of consciousness. You could ask yourself, each time you notice it, who *is* this "I"?

As Self-realization clarifies, it becomes obvious that the I-thought is at the root of our confusion and suffering. For the latter part to end, there must be a change in the former part: from self to Self. This doesn't mean that we no longer use the word *I*, but we do not lose sight of *who* that I *is*.

Is that *I* present in your deepest sleep? If not, do such troubling concerns arise?

In the Fire

The vital essence of nonduality so eludes the average, conditioned mind that would-be transmitters of it have spent decades of their life and succeeded in communicating it to only a few of their listeners.

Why? Because the listener expects to remain intact while undergoing a "transcendent," *trans-personal* process!

The consequence of the nondual realization is that the "person" dies as an identifiable entity to him/herself. The "listener" who sets out on this discovery *does not* remain intact, as a recognized entity, beyond the point of real-ization!

It is this unwillingness to die to one's self-identity which makes nonduality unrealizable.

Our *dualistic*, conditioned point of view makes it possible (indeed, necessary) for our self-identity to remain as a so-called reality. Hence, "I" become united with "God": God continues to exist as God—a separate entity; and I continue to exist as a self-identifiable "person." God = a unit. I = a unit. Two units. Duality.

What Bernadette Roberts is referring to is burning up, as a coal, in the fire of God; *and* the fire of God evaporating into the ether of unspecified beingness. No longer a "God," no longer a "person." Not a first unit, and a second unit, but a condition (a presence, really) which exhibits no residue of God, no residue of you. No unit which represents something that is, in any way, apart from its co-relator. No object and no subject.

That is the substance of the nondual realization: that there is but a *singular* actuality. Being a singular actuality, not anything *else* is it, *but* it. Ergo, there not *being* anything else which is it, *it* is *all things* which appear to exist.

Being *all that is*, it is (among everything else) the very mind which realizes! It is, in effect, reifying itself; "it" is existent—by being real-ized in "our" awareness.

Being all that is, it is not only your mind and my mind (*whether or not* that mind reflects its true nature), but it is "you" and "me" in any way in which we perceive our "self" (body, thoughts, emotions, actions, etc. etc.).

So, the realized are in recognition of their true identity: Absolute Presence; Beingness.

Every and all entities (forms; "things") are subsumed in this one, over-extending actuality: this is the nondual realization.

When all things are *That*, not only are you and I That, but every other human (or animate; *in*animate too!) form, equally as well. No body that has ever breathed earthly air is any different from you in this regard, in being That— our common denominator.

No one has ever been *closer* to That than you are at this very moment. You are That. (Drop the "you" and the "That" if you really cognize the point being made.)

To the extent that you (and "others") are That, you are not who you think you are. Recognizing the truth of this, your false *self*-identity falls away, like an adder drops its skin. The old "person"-ality *dies*.

Parts Unknown

The two matters you're asking about are related. If there ever was an enigma, it would be the matter of what the mystics are attempting to describe as "nothingness." Anything said about it is an unintended koan. And yet, it is the very mystery which every seeker is ultimately seeking.

The query "how does *something* arise from *nothing*" can be an opening gambit.

From the standpoint of *ajata* ("no creation")—*The* most fundamental of teachings—there *is* no arising.

Nothingness is meant to mean exactly what it *is*. Nothing. It is not, therefore, the opposite of somethingness.

Somethingness is customarily a catchword for the "relative": things, material or immaterial. Nothingness is a word often associated with the "absolute." An actual meaning of absolute is "not relative": not *a thing*; no thing; nothing.

But, as used in the above sense, the Absolute is said to be an *aspect* of all that is relative; and all that is relative is said to be an *aspect* of the ("all-inclusive") Absolute. In other words, the actual identity of both conditions is the same.

So, if something (relative) is nothing (Absolute), while at the same time nothing is something, the two categories cancel each other out.

We could say that "what remains" is the nothingness, as alluded to by the (bedrock) nondual teaching called ajata.

In other words, it is truly beyond conception.

As a baby, pre-cognitive, you knew nothing about nothingness; put another way, you knew as much about nothingness as is to be known.

In fact, what you knew about nothingness was as much as you knew about your "self": and that was all you needed to know about yourself. So, your first "I am" was superimposed on that emptiness of identification.

With the arising of our first (even though natural) "self" identification, we began our limited identity as *something*.

We give names to the various conditions or aspects of ice: cold, heavy, solid, crystalline, brittle, wet, slippery, glassy, clear, dense, changeable, etc. But beneath all the classifications, it's simply ice.

We could say "I am." We could say, I am this: _____. We could say, "I am That." All of it is the arising of an image, of some-thing-ness. The use of the idiom nothingness is meant to be a background upon which we can notice the "arising" of the naming of some thing, such as *I*.

Death: The Mystical Advent

An atom is, as the dictionary puts it, "a complex arrangement of electrons revolving about a nucleus which contains protons, neutrons and other particles." There is, of course, a universal order to this revolving, complex arrangement; it is not chaotic, and is consistent from atom to atom. In its role in the formation of matter, we could say that it is "*in*formed." Indeed, given the extent of its complex arrangement of revolutions, it can be considered an intelligent form, or element, of life. In fact, the entire subatomic network appears to be "alive," to many physicists—as the cosmos appears to be, to many astronomers.

When an atom combines with other atoms to form a molecule, the atomic "information"—which results in its orderly, "intelligent" behavior—is passed along to the molecule. When these molecules orchestrate with other molecules to form our body, the innate informed intelligence, or "wisdom," does not absent itself from our body: it is the source of wound healing and other orderings of the body. Its capacity for ordering, in fact, goes at least as far back as the gestation which occurs when sperm meets ovum. And, of course, in the sperm and ovum itself this same intelligent ordering has proceeded heretofore.

When this innate intelligence, following its own pattern of ordering, closes down the vital functions of the body, the body expires ("breathe out"). The molecules begin an orderly breakdown, and the body reverts to organic elements—minerals or other atomic constituents—in the earth, sea or air. These elements are freed to again combine in another form. For example, they may be leached up into a tree where they become the components of fruit; this fruit may be eaten by a gatherer, where they become components of her ovum. But what we might call the innate "consciousness" of the atom has remained invariably intact throughout all evolving stages.

At one of these stages, the informed interactions of the atoms and molecules, and their variety of elements, have combined to form our brain; in addition to our innate body wisdom, we now have a capacity for thought—through which, you might say, the collective atomic consciousness has the ability to be conscious of itself.

This portion of the entire field of consciousness, which now is conscious of itself as a unit or individual (a word which originally was synonymous with "indivisible"), we call the self (whose root originally meant "a-part"): the collection of "conscious" body particles are now "self conscious."

When the body expires and the brain ceases to function, the process reverses: the body's collective (self) consciousness dissipates as the collection of molecules and atoms revert to their individualized conditions in the disassembling of the unitary body. But the unchanged intelligence or consciousness in each atomic particle remains unaffected, to create new elements.

For the sake of our discussion, so far, we have spoken of the atoms as if they were discrete units, with the information or intelligence of each contained "within" it, as if the atoms were building blocks similar to grains of sand. However, as scientists peer closely at the atom, they recognize that it actually represents a non-material *pattern*—such as a vortex in water—and that these patterns overlap each other, similar to the way that waves behave on water...arising and subsiding. Indeed, the very subatomic particles of your body—as you read this—are in interaction with the particle-patterns in the air which presses down upon you, and with the table upon which you rest your hand, etc.: yet each pattern is maintaining, at this time, the integrity with which it is presently informed. In other words, part of the intelligent operation is that the particle-patterns can mix, without getting mixed-up. And, yet, there is nothing *physically material* about them to keep them distinct (in fact, most of their composition is what appears to us as empty space).

The point of this is that all of these subatomic particles are in ceaseless *interaction* with other particle-patterns—right throughout the entire material and nonmaterial universe. And in the same way that the atoms do *not* maintain discrete individuality, their "information" or intelligence is likewise cohesively *communal*. In other words, in the way in which your body is connected to—or a consequence of—the collective intelligence of its composite atoms, so too are the atoms connected to, or a consequence of, the field by which their order and interaction coherently arises. To put it another way, the "consciousness" of the atom(s) is "cosmic consciousness": the order of each and all is in no way apart from the order of the universe or its source.

This is important to recognize, because this is essentially what the mystic sages mean when they say that our personalized consciousness arises from, and returns to, a field or source of universal or omnipresent, impersonal consciousness. (Buddha-mind, to Buddhists).

Furthermore, this universal source or repository of consciousness is not inert; it is alive in the very *expression* of activity of the atomic substrate which composes all *living* matter (capable of individual movement). And, through our brains (at least), it is not only conscious, but even self conscious of its own presence or actuality.

And, so, it was from an "alive" field that your body came into life: there was no point at which any of its constituents were dead (incapable of movement or activity)—although generic *self* consciousness may pass, eternally, from being to being. A drop of water, taken from the pond, contains living matter; returned to the pond, it is the pond's life.

The reason why it is so important to recognize this is because it is not consciousness which comes and goes, it is the body (and its "self" consciousness) which comes and goes—is born and dies. *Consciousness* itself, as the sages put it, is unborn and undying—present everywhere at all times.

This brings us to some of the more practical implications, concerning "death."

This consciousness, which is unborn and undying, is your very consciousness—you can have no consciousness without, or apart from, it. Its consciousness of its self—as a particular energy pattern, similar to a vortex—is person-alized, as each "self" arises (is formed) and expires. "Self" consciousness arises with the creation of the body and expires with the destruction of the body: but the consciousness itself existed, in a "less personalized" form, before the formation of the body—and will be present afterward. Your consciousness now, we might say, is merely a personalized form, for the moment, of universal consciousness. To put this another way, it is the body which can die, because it is only the body which was born.

What we are saying, from this point, is of course necessarily speculative. But what follows ought to be obvious, from a consistent point of view.

The first implicit factor of death is that you will not know that you have died—because you haven't.

At the point of physical death, you will only be aware that there has been a bodily, physical change. You will not be aware of a change of consciousness, because it is only consciousness of the body which is undergoing change; consciousness itself has no need, no purpose, to change. You will be objectively aware that the body is inert and incapable of independent activity. You will be aware that this consciousness has maintained an association with the body; but your awareness will be that the consciousness is not dependent upon the body. In that sense, you will be aware that consciousness is not limited; and in that sense, there will be awareness that That Which Is Conscious Is That Which Is Unlimited. The "you" which is aware is an impersonal you.

That which, "in" the body, was aware of its self, is aware of itself still—as *unlimited*. And in this complete absorption, it now loses awareness of itself as a thing. Consciousness "returns," wholly and indistinguishable, to the field from which it continually "arises" anew, in each unique, personalized form.

This field has no location; it is not set off somewhere, apart: it is omnipresent. Therefore, it is not really accurate to say that consciousness "returns"; there is no "where" to which it can return, nor is there a where from which it arose: it is, in fact, always present. This means that there is no "place" where your consciousness "settles," upon death. It also means that, from the standpoint of your consciousness, there is no such reality as death.

This is not a denial of "personal" death; it is to say that that which is personal is impermanent—arises and expires—but that which is conscious of the "person" and its "personality" is unaffected by the objects of which it is conscious. This consciousness—which is our common consciousness—was present before each person's birth and will be persistent throughout the change we call death.

The person known as Ramana Maharshi died of cancer. On the last day, when his disciples were gathering around his dying body, one cried out, "Master, please don't leave us!"

"Leave you!", the sage replied, "Where could I go?!"

*

On the death of any living creature, the spirit returns to the spiritual world, the body to the bodily world. In this, however, only the bodies are subject to change. The spiritual world is one single spirit, who stands like unto a light behind the bodily world; and who, when any single creature comes into being, shines through it, as through a window. According to the kind and size of the window, less or more light enters the world. The light itself however remains unchanged.

– Persian mystic Aziz Nasafi (Thirteenth Century)

Presence of Being

The persistent question for some seekers is, "If 'I am That', why do I not sense it, or know it?"

You are doubtless *objectifying* it. As a subject (you), there is an attempt to relate to it as some thing, somehow apart: "I am *this* thing; it is *that* thing."

It is vital to recognize that it is not a thing; any *thing* has a confining limitation as the basis of its particular definition: it is the thing it is, within the boundary of all that it is not. But the referent, here, is posited by all traditions to be boundless, without limitation whatsoever. As such, it must also be without configuration, without form of any kind.

Being formless, it is not an *object*; all objects are forms limited by boundaries. Consequently, it cannot be exclusively seen, touched, heard or apprehended by sensory apparatus, in any way. Nor can it be known as we would know any other element or object or form. All that can be *realized* is its true ineffable circumstance.

All referent suggestions of its circumstances say: infinite (titling it sometimes as Infinite), eternal (Eternal), and without limitation: unrestrained spatially, unconfined temporally, ever present every where, without being limited as a form anywhere.

It is sometimes said to be the background, or the ground of being, in which all forms are present. Your form, as a limited organism, "rests" on this ground as a "human" *being*. Your being is within, or an element of, Its being.

Whenever you acknowledge—are aware of—*your* being, you are in recognition of Its being. Its "being" is not apart from *being*: there is no subject (me) / object (It) *relationship* here. Therefore, you cannot—as a subject (me)—attempt to sense or know it objectively, as *separate* from your self. To the extent that you are aware of the presence of the subject-you, you are aware of the presence of It (*as* the subject).

It is as much your being as the "being" that you think of as your (form of) self. Whatever action "you" take, it is Being activated. In—or as—one limited form over here (you), an action is taken. In, or as, another limited form over there (me), I take another particular action. Every form that is manifest within its field is expressing an aspect of the presence of Being.

Your awareness (as subject) is an aspect of Being; what you are aware of (as object) is an aspect of Being. When you are aware of (the form of) an idea, (the form of) a concept, (the form of) a thought, a form of Being is aware of a form of Being. Actions that are consequently taken (or avoided) are a form of Being.

Being is the actor, the action and the acted upon, impartial to all manifest occurrences as the formless—and *itself* inactive—presence or enabling condition.

Some organisms that we call individuals are constantly aware of this Presence of being. Some are not. This presence is no more absent in those who are *not* aware of it, than in those who *are* aware of it. Whether the inclination to be aware of it has expressed as a circumstance in one organism, while not in another, is of no consequence to the condition of Presence: it is impartially ever-present in every case.

Whether one contemplates these matters, and a qualitative development in awareness occurs, makes no difference in any ultimate sense. All forms that arise will eventually subside, so nothing that is thought, said or done will have any impressive effect on the eternal Being.

Therefore, if you don't sense or know "I am That," it is not a matter for concern to present awareness. If there is, on the other hand, self-awareness as Being present, the "self" that is aware of it will not experience it as I (*subject*) am That (*object*), in any case, but as the *dis*appearance of both subject and object.

Settling for Less

J.D.:

As to your first question: read the lives of the spiritual exemplars; poverty has not been a barrier to a Self-realized life. In fact, it can be an aid. Fear is a much bigger barrier.

Second question: to the extent that you identify yourself as a Muslim or Sufi, you are not free to embrace your *unlimited* identity. Self-realization has nothing to do with obeying the dictates of an external authority. Your sheikh may be able to tell you what you should, or should not, do within the confines of Islam; but the freedom of illumination in Self-realization is sure to elude you as long as you settle for shop-worn conventions.

Not Knowing

The realization, which one has in Self-realization, is not an experience. And, contrary to being a "knowing," it is an un-knowing.

The reason why this can be said is because Self-realization is merely a profound insight into the total and complete absence of limitation. In other words, it is entirely outside the bounds of both experience and knowledge.

In fact, to the Self-realized, the word which comes closest (to the condition described above) is *nothingness*.

In actuality, it is not a matter of "knowing Oneness" or "experiencing sublime consciousness." It is an irrepressible realization that the ultimate condition is of no-thing; nothing.

In other words, in this absolute awareness there is not anything about which we suppose we will be certain, as a conceiver knows a concept.

It may sound peculiar, but this is the Self-realized state.

World To-Do List

"What is one to do about all the ills in the world?"

That has been the central question in *my* life. And I can't answer that for you; only for myself.

At age sixteen, I read Dale Carnegie's *How to Win Friends and Influence People*. World War II and Auschwitz were still fresh in people's mind; and even *then* your question had occurred to me. So, I was interested to know: How can I influence anyone to be more peaceful?

In my mid-twenties I was involved in the radical end of the peace movement (the nonviolent activists inspired by Gandhi's and Martin Luther King's social change): we might be engaged in an anti-draft rally in front of an Army recruitment center, say, and be harangued by a group of self-appointed "patriots," who knew that we were pacifists—and they weren't. I came to recognize that they were motivated by *ideals*, just as *we* were. I also concluded, through studying world history, that our social problems were not going to be eradicated through politics or religion, both of which are basically self-serving.

I began to notice that where people's behavior is dictated by outward constraints, such as laws or armed force, they will revert back to their preferred behaviors as soon as the pressure is removed. Only when a person is acting out of his own heartfelt desire will he *eagerly continue*, in the course of action *chosen*.

In my thirties, I began to study Zen Buddhism because I sensed that enlightenment is basically a change of heart at a fundamental level; and that, historically, enlightenment has proven to find its expression in compassionate behavior. My interest eventually (in my fifties) led to my own spiritual awakening: and, indeed, to a profound change of heart, noticed in my change in values and in my behavior toward all others.

The natural question which arises when one undergoes a benign shift in consciousness is, "How can the life-changing shift, that I've experienced, be communicated to others?"

First of all, is this possible? I have proven to myself that it is. And so I dedicated the balance of my life to this objective: social change (if there is to be any), one person at a time, one heart at a time.

So, my answer to what one is to do, about the world's ills, is to (first) awaken to the life-changing truth that is known as Self-realization; and (second) assist others in discovering that personal change of heart.

That's my answer to the question, on the relative level. But from the standpoint of a person once Self-realized, this question takes on an even deeper significance. And the answer to this question is not likely to be comprehensible to other than the Self-realized person.

There is a fundamentally different view of our world from the standpoint of enlightenment, as contrasted to the perspective of dualism. This is summarized by a comment of Ramana Maharshi: "So long as identification with the body ('I') lasts, the world seems to be outside us."

In other words, to the "individual" mind, there is "me" and all else that is "not me"; among the things we conclude are not-me are "the world" (or cosmos).

That the "world" is a concept, or idea, is plain: in deep sleep, both the perception of a me *and* the world are entirely absent. As Ramana puts it,

> "It is only the 'individual' mind that sees the world. When this mind disappears, the world also disappears.... The world appears when you wake up (from sleep). So where is it? Clearly, the world (awake or dreaming) is in your thought.... The mirror reflects objects; yet they are not real, because they cannot remain apart from the mirror. Similarly, the world is said to be a 'reflection in the mind', as it does not remain in the absence of mind."

Consider: if there were no conscious minds, would there be anything to say that there was such an independent construct as a "world"?

So, how does the enlightened perceive what, in dualistic terms, is referred to as the world? From the perspective of nonduality, there is only one, indivisible actuality: the Absolute (or Ramana's term, Self; to others, God). Therefore, there exists no individuated, part-icularized "me," nor conceived "not-me." When we come to realize the truth of this cosmic viewpoint, this is called "Self-realization"; you know who or what "you" are: no thing. When the 'I'—as subject (or seer)—is shown to have no validity, the conception of "separate" objects is also deconstructed.

"Find out what *you* are, and then you understand what the world is," Ramana points out.

> "Duality of subject and objects are your *thought* creations.... Do you not (nightly) create a world in

your dream? The waking state (in which you 'see' the 'world') is also a long, drawn-out dream."

This might be summarized as: the world is as real as a dream; a dream is an illusion. To realize the "true nature" of the "world," one must first realize that the true nature of both you (and all "others") *and* the world is the Absolute (Self).

Ramana: "If we first know the Self, then all other matters will be plain to us....Therefore, one must know the Self, before the world is known."

Here is the nub of what Self-realization tells us: if the true nature of *all* seers is the Absolute, then both those who see the world as "real" and those who don't are equally a manifested activity of (or by) the Absolute. The former is concerned about the existence, or activities, regarding the world; the latter does not recognize the world, or its activities, to be other than the Absolute.

Thus Ramana says:

> "The world is created by the 'I', which in its turn arises from the Self.... The unenlightened takes the world to be real, whereas the enlightened sees it only as a manifestation of the Self. So then it becomes immaterial whether the Self *manifests* itself, or *ceases* to do so [as a 'world'].... The Self is infinite, inclusive of all that you see. There is nothing beyond it, nor apart from it.... The power which has created you has created the world. If it can take care of you, it can similarly take care of the world, also."

This is what has been said as "*Thy* will, be done."

And, here, we come to the potentiality for peace in the relative world: the nonattachment which allows the 'what is' to *be* what it *is*.

Ramana said to someone who was highly agitated about the affairs of the world, "Can you stop the wars, or reform the world?"

"No."

"Then why worry yourself about what is not possible for you?"

What, then, are we to do?

> "First set yourself right, and *then only* set out to improve 'others'. Change the *hearts* of men, and the *world* will surely change. But one must begin somewhere, and one can begin only with oneself.... When one is not oneself at peace, how can that one spread peace in the world?... When the Self is known, all 'others' become known. Self-realization is, hence, the primary—and sole—duty of mankind."

Myth as Religion

The methodology that we call science is relatively new in human history. Compare it to mankind's ten-times longer quest to discover the nature of what was categorized as "spirit."

But in the brief span since Galileo's day, science has cast revealing light on the subject which has immemorially been referred to as the Absolute. For example, no intelligent person believes, today, that a Deity created our planet, and its environs, less than five thousand years ago.

A reassessment of the "heavens and earth" has been sudden and dramatic. At the beginning of the 20th Century, we knew that the universe comprised more than our sun and its nine planets visible to us. But still it was believed that our galaxy of stars was the extent of the universe. Today, we know that there are untold billions of galaxies inhabiting the universe, containing countless planetary solar systems akin to our own. Belief in a Jehovah, who labored only seven days and was satisfied with one solar system, is no longer credible.

People are no longer entering churches, synagogues, temples, mosques or cathedrals in hope of coming face-to-face with anything that's divine; presumed priestly intermediaries are now expected only to dole out old-fashioned morals and unrealistic ethics.

Yet the quest to personally know the truth of ultimate reality is unabated. Such knowledge is being sought outside of any self-identified religious institution. And what such institutions have persistently been incapable of delivering, is being discovered by increasing numbers of inquirers whose intent is not persuasively sublimated by saccharine scriptures.

Anyone, who is rational enough to know that climate change is not God's punishment for the sanctioning of gay marriage, is capable of understanding the precepts of Self-realization—which has satisfied spiritual seekers in every time and place for millennia.

Modern scientific inquiry has been an asset to sincere spiritual inquirers; and it has been a demolisher of the ancient tribal superstitions that we know today as religions.

Myth is not truth. Truth is not myth.

Always Present

According to an eight-page biography of Bankei Yotaku (1622-93), in *The Roaring Stream*, this son of a samurai began Zen study at age 16, and was enlightened at age 25. He seriously began teaching Zen ten years later; and fifteen years after that, he became abbot of a monastery. By age 55, he was being sought out, by both male and female seekers of the Dharma, from all over Japan—and even from Okinawa. The reason apparently had much to do with the fact that he was not "practice" oriented.

Though he didn't like his talks to be transcribed, some were preserved by followers. Here then are various of his points (as given in the book).

What he calls the "Unborn" and "buddha-mind" are alternate terms. He is speaking of the pre-cognitive "wisdom" that is innate in each human organism which is born; it is prior to our acquiring discursive thought. His purpose is to remind listeners that there is not something which they must do in order for this buddha-mind to "come into existence," or be present.

> "Just stop and look back to the origin of this self of yours. When you were born, your parents didn't give you any happy, evil, or bitter thoughts. There was only your buddha-mind...What I teach everyone in these talks of mine is the unborn buddha-mind of illuminative wisdom, nothing else. Everyone is endowed with this buddha-mind, only they don't know it. My reason for coming and speaking to you like this is to make it known to you."

He means our perception which does not distinguish, in terms of the "self"; it senses the world which the body experiences, without qualifying, or critiquing, whatever is sensed. It is the facility by which we walk, without having to think about taking steps. Our actions can be performed without the need to have any *ideas* about how they are to be performed: without thinking that "I am a man," it is a man acting; without the need to think "I am a woman," there is a woman moving.

> "That you see and hear and smell in this way, without giving rise to the *thought* that *you* will, is the proof that this inherent buddha-mind is unborn and possessed of a wonderful illuminative wisdom... When you're walking along naturally, you're walking in the harmony of the Unborn...The place in which there's no difference in the hearing of sounds is the Unborn, the buddha-mind, and it's perfectly equal and absolutely the same in each one of you. When we say 'This is a man', or 'This is a woman', those are designations that result from the arising of *thought*; they come afterward. At the place of the Unborn, *before* the thought arises, attributes such as 'man' or 'woman' don't even exist."

The Unborn buddha-mind did not originate at some point when we began giving *attention* to it. We were born into the presence of the buddha-mind. Nor is it something which we can lose or vacate. Qualitative, or discriminatory, thoughts which occur to us ("I am a woman") are *superimposed* upon the underlying, or innate, buddha-mind. The buddha-mind is ever-present; qualitative thoughts, defining "attributes," are sometimes also present as well.

"The reason I say it's in the 'Unborn' that you see and hear, in this way, is because the mind doesn't give 'birth' to any thought or *inclination* to see or hear. Therefore it is *un-born*. Being Unborn, it's also undying: *it's not possible for what is not born to perish*. This is the sense in which I say that all people have an unborn buddha-mind...You see, *you are always unborn:* you go along living in the buddha-mind quite unconscious of being a man or woman. But while you are doing that, perhaps you'll happen to see or hear something that bothers you; perhaps someone will make a nasty remark about you, saying they don't like you, or whatever. You let your mind fasten onto that, you begin to fret over it, and thoughts crowd into your mind."

Should we, then, follow a discipline for stilling this mind, or emptying the mind of its contents?

"I won't tell you that you have to practice such and such, that you have to uphold certain rules or precepts, or read certain sutras or other Zen writings, or that you have to do zazen...You can grasp your buddha-mind very easily, right where you sit, without that long, painstaking practice."

His teaching was carefully explained, to a listener who stated: "Someone like me, who hasn't engaged in any practice or arrived at any enlightenment, couldn't possibly achieve true peace of mind simply by perceiving the necessity of living in the unborn buddha-mind, and staying just as I am." Bankei:

"It's like this. A group of travelers, climbing through a stretch of high mountains, gets thirsty; and one of them strikes out and makes his way far down into the valley to fetch water. It's not easy, but he finally finds some, and brings it back and gives his companions a drink. Don't those who drink, without having exerted themselves, quench their thirst the same as the one who did? Now, if a person refused to drink the water because he felt that doing it was wrong, there wouldn't be any way to quench his thirst."

"My own struggle was undertaken *mistakenly*, because I didn't happen to meet up with a clear-eyed master: Eventually, though, I discovered the buddha-mind for myself; ever since, I have been telling others about theirs, so they'll know about it without going through that ordeal; just as those people drink water and quench their thirst, without having to go and find it for themselves."

Yes, but aren't the thoughts of some people "deluded"?

Deluded thoughts could only be the product of, or consequence of, not recognizing that all discursive thoughts are merely appearances in the presence of the Unborn buddha-mind. Deluded, or illusory, thoughts are simply one, of the number of varieties, of discursive thoughts.

A disciple: "I don't question that there are no illusory thoughts in the primary mind; but just the same, there's no let-up to the thoughts that keep coming into *my* mind. I find it impossible to *stay in* the Unborn." Bankei:

"Although you arrived in the world with *nothing but* the unborn buddha-mind, you fell into your present deluded ways as you were growing up, by watching and listening to other people in their delusion. You picked all this up gradually, over a long period of time, habituating *your mind* to it, until now your deluded mind has taken over completely and works its delusion, unchecked. But none of those deluded thoughts of yours was inborn. They weren't there from the start. *They came to exist* in a mind that's originally the *Unborn*."

What is one to do, if delusive thoughts are recognized to exist?

A monk:

"I have a great difficulty subduing all the desires, and deluded thoughts, in my mind. What should I do?" Bankei: "The idea to *subdue* deluded thoughts *is* a deluded thought itself. None of those thoughts exist from the start. You conjure them up out of your own *discriminations*."

Typically, a deluded thought would be to conclude that you need to *concern* yourself about some particular variety of thought which occurs in the presence of the Unborn buddha-mind—or, additionally, fret about whether or not there are deluded thoughts that may occur *elsewhere* in the human population. Such are worries that you conjure up "out of your own discriminations." The Unborn buddha-mind is not affected by such self-concerns.

To a follower, he said: "Illusory thoughts are no different. If you just *let them come and let them go away*, and don't put them to work or try to *avoid* them, then one day you'll find that they've vanished completely into the Unborn mind."

So, need you stew over the nature of your thoughts?

A disciple: "Every time I clear a thought from my mind, another appears right away. Thoughts keep appearing like that, without end. What can I do about them?" Bankei:

> "Clearing thoughts from the mind as they arise is like washing away blood in blood...Since you don't know that your mind is originally Unborn (and undying and free of illusion) you think that your thoughts really exist....You have to realize that your thoughts are ephemeral and unreal and, without either *clutching at them or rejecting them*, just let them come and go of themselves."

Bankei taught that "the marvelous illumination of the Unborn buddha-mind deals perfectly with every possible situation," which must include vagrant thoughts.

The Unborn buddha-mind does not declare that some development ought to go "this way," and not "that way."

And considering that everyone who sees, hears, smells or walks is engaged in the buddha-mind, one who recognizes this does not presume that some particular activity brings a person closer to it, or that some lack of activity takes a person further away from it.

The Unborn buddha-mind is not some special state which one acquires by means of one's desire to do so; it is unavoidable, in that we are born into it. Bankei emphasizes this repeatedly. Some are aware that their thoughts and activities arise within a sphere of innate and pre-cognitive wisdom, and some are not aware.

Those abiding in the Unborn mind have no reason to be disturbed about the outcome either way; *abiding* means to "go on being," without categorizing—aware that "All things are perfectly resolved in the Unborn."

"Our Father Who Art..."

Your question: "Is there a God? Yes or no?"

No. Not in the sense that your question implies. Most everyone who uses that term conceives of a God as an entity, a form; yet, at the same time, most persons would say that God is *omnipresent*. If so, God would not be a form among other forms, but would be present *in* the same space in which every other form was present; in other words, would occupy every form (from the inside out).

As such there would be no form which limited It, or contained it; It would be beyond, or transcendent of, any form. Unlimited by any constraint of form, it would not itself be an entity.

The nondual teachings, therefore, call it form-less; also Absolute, which means "not limited."

"Does it exist or not exist, then?"

For those who suppose that God is an entity, they would then of course posit that this God has existence. The nondual teachings speak of the Absolute as neither existent nor non-existent. That which is omnipresent, in other words is not finite, does not come into existence (as a form) or go out of existence. From another view, being without *limitation*, It would be non-existent *as well as* existent.

As the Vedas suggest, if the question was (instead of God) "Does the Absolute exist?", the sage would have no argument with those who maintain no; yes; both; or neither.

The Middle Way

By some dint of fate...Tenzin Palmo, as Khamtrul Rinpoche's 'only nun', managed to find herself in the bizarre situation of being a lone woman among 100 monks. By absolute accident, she had entered the mighty portals of Tibetan monasticism, barred to the opposite sex for centuries.

Later, Tenzin Palmo was to remark pointedly: 'People are always asking me how they can give up anger, but no one has yet asked me how to give up desire.'

(Cave in the Snow)

Do you see the point made by this nun (Diane Perry of London), in her biography? While the monks and the nun were working on ending such compulsions as their anger, they also had to deal with such tensions as sexual desire.

In other words, you are concerned as to how to curb your emotions which create *pain*. You are not asking how to curb such emotions as those which create *pleasure*, such as joy.

Her point is that it is desire which needs to be defused: the desire to *avoid* pain, and the desire to *seek* pleasure; or, the effort to change dissatisfaction into satisfaction.

The teachings of nonduality are pointing toward equanimity. *And* they are emphasizing the absence of personhood. Where there is no 'I', there is no beneficiary for sustained joy. Where there is no I, there is no personage lessened by an expression of anger. Where there is no I, there is not a preference for one condition over the other.

The Sage and Illness

Yes, Hope, your question is rarely addressed in the spiritual literature, because it is so difficult for the ajnani (un-realized) to grapple with.

As Ramana says, all of the relative forms are impermanent. There is only one thing which does not come and go, which is permanent, and that is the ground of being, or Source. He says, "Keep attention focused on what is real, what does not come and go, not on what is unreal" (that is, impermanent).

The human body is impermanent. What it (and the entire cosmos) owes its existence to is, as the sutras say, "unchanging," ever-present. Human forms appear and disappear, in limited time and space, within it; but It does not vary in its presence, and is not limited in time or space.

So, the *jnani's* attention is focused on the ultimate Reality, not the short-lived forms through which this Reality merely makes an appearance. Thus the sutras emphasize, "*You* are not the body."

In specific terms, the jnani (through choiceless awareness) observes changes which are taking place within the organism (and "*all* things change"), recognizing that a physical body will necessarily follow the course of arriving, remaining, and departing.

You used the word "illness" (as would most persons), but in the sage's mind what is noticed is "change." Change is inevitable; change which eventually leads to death is emphatically inevitable.

The usual human reaction to change, especially when life-threatening, is resistance. For one to whom the self and the Self are one indivisible whole, where is there a basis for resistance?

In *Living Nonduality* (p. 224: How They Died), I wrote of the "non-resistance to physical death" of four exemplary spiritual teachers: the concluding line speaks about "non-attachment to life itself," that is, to *all* that is impermanent.

About Nothing

I suppose you could say, Tenzin, the Heart Sutra is to the Diamond Sutra, as ajata is to advaita.

While both speak of emptiness, the context of the Diamond Sutra uses various "things"—world, self, thoughts, etc.—to *elaborate* on their emptiness, their lack of "intrinsic existence" from the standpoint of ultimate reality.

The Heart Sutra more clearly points out that the essence of *emptiness*, as ultimate reality, is that there's nothing to talk *about*—world, self, thought, etc.—where there is neither "existence" nor "nonexistence" from the very start.

But both of these pillars of Buddhism are hardly understood, even by those who chant sutras daily.

To clarify the above, I'll excerpt from two monographs of mine.

The Diamond Sutra first, in which Buddha converses with disciple Subhuti.

One translator suggests that the Buddha spoke on this sutra's subject matter circa 400 B.C., and emphasized "emptiness is the true nature of reality."

Buddha states that those who "gain perfect clarity of mind" (enlightenment), "do not create the perception of a self. Nor do they create the perception of a being, a life...."

But this self-identity is normally a continuous one in our thoughts. In the enlightened sage's thoughts, from moment to moment, he (or she) does not "create"—or re-create—this erroneous perception. In other words, he is "empty" of such—and similar—false perceptions, and this results in "perfect clarity of mind."

In fact, all "things," every thing, is similarly and equally empty of reality, because dharma is transcendent of "thingness"; by its nature, it is undifferentiated. So, that which dharma transcends – all things – are "unreal"; only the transcendent dharma has (is) reality.

Therefore, even Buddha is unreal, to the extent that he is viewed as some thing; or, in particular, as a "self." Likewise he would not, either, be a "being," as an entity; consequently it could not be said that he had a "life."

The emptiness of things applies to conceived things, as well as substantial or material things. The (insubstantial) "self" is merely the prime example. To even say that there is such a thing as "existence," on the one hand, or "nonexistence," is to make a differentiation which has no reality from the standpoint of dharma.

Thus, Buddha says, in this sutra, "In the dharma (reality) realized and taught and reflected on" by him (the Tathagata), "there is nothing true and nothing false." He cannot claim any such thing.

"The Buddha said...neither can someone who creates the perception of a life [his or others'], or even the perception of a soul [or afterlife], be called a bodhisattva." He emphasizes, "No beginning [and thus no finite ending], Subhuti, is the highest truth."

Where there is no such thing as a self, there is no self which perceives a "world."

Where there is no self, there is no thinker who creates differentiated perceptions, or thoughts. "Subhuti, a past thought cannot be found. A future thought cannot be found. Nor can a present thought be found."

"Subhuti," said Buddha, "undifferentiated is this dharma, in which nothing (no thing) is differentiated."

And he said, as "an illusion...a bubble, a dream....view all 'created' things like this."

Subhuti comprehended: "Bhagavan, if a universe existed, attachment to an entity would exist."

"The Buddha said....foolish people, though, are attached."

He advised that each discover "the self-less, birthless nature" of reality; renounce "self existence every day"; "and master this entire teaching, and explain it in detail to others. For in that place, Subhuti, dwells a teacher or one who represents the guru of wisdom."

And Subhuti states: "Sages arise from what is uncreated."

> "Subhuti, those who are called 'tathagatas' do not go anywhere, nor do they come from anywhere. Thus they are called 'tathagata, fully-enlightened ones.'"

*

Let's look at the Heart Sutra.

Any phenomena which is considered to exist—material, such as objects/forms, or immaterial, such as conceptions or events—are characterized as "things,"through a multiplicity of "differences." Without defining "characteristics" there could not be said to be any particular "thing." Therefore, all phenomena are devoid of (or empty of) defining characteristics "naturally": differences are not intrinsic to any elements which share existence, but are imposed upon them by the human mind. Undefined existence has no independent "characteristics." It is merely a universal Presence, or Totality. It is simply "empty" of definite qualities. Absent of any named appearances, is a Void.

However, due to our relativistic tendency, our normal inclination is to visualize the Unnamed and Unnameable as contra-distinctive from those elements we have named or that are nameable. In so doing, we counterpose that which has no independent existence to all those things to which we have given relative reality, or existence—thus we ineluctably transmute "emptiness" into just another relative thing.

In other words, forms and formlessness are inseparable in either their purported existence or their nonexistence. There is a qualification, however. We bring the forms into existence. Emptiness cannot even have the defining characteristic of existence. All conceived forms have a beginning and an ending, as contrasted with emptiness.

The setting of the Heart Sutra's account is a visit by the Buddha to a community of adherents at a place called Vulture Peak. His disciple Avalokiteshvara is saying to disciple Shariputra, with Buddha's agreement, "Form is emptiness, emptiness is form...Therefore, Shariputra, in emptiness there is no form...Likewise, there is no origin, cessation, or path..."

In a commentary on the Heart Sutra, the Dalai Lama has said:

> "Emptiness constitutes the highest and most subtle understanding of the Buddha's teaching on no-self... and this is a crucial point: even emptiness itself is devoid of intrinsic existence....

"Thus, meditative practice is negated. Next, the fruition of this practice is negated—'there is no wisdom, no attainment'—by affirming the emptiness of the subjective experience...All the qualities of the mind of one who has reached nirvana...these are empty, and are negated here...Thus the emptiness of the mind is said to be the basis of nirvana, it's natural nirvana....Emptiness is therefore both the means of eliminating the mental afflictions [confusion] and the resultant state that one arrives at after having done so."

So, this is important for you to recognize, as a "Buddhist"; The empty mind does not make a distinction between relative awareness ("defiled") and enlightened awareness ("undefiled"): both are without existence independent of the mind, or thought. The realized views both the relative and that which is not relative as the same in all that is witnessed. In emptiness, there is not anything to be "left out" or excluded. Awareness of the relative does not obscure awareness of the non-relative, and vice versa.

You can see here, then, that the central emphasis of both these foundational sutras is emptiness or nothingness, or ultimate non-existence. This also relates to the teachings of no-self (nor other-than-self: "not two") of advaita, and the even more pronounced teaching—sometimes referred to as ajata (definition: no creation)—that there has not been any thing "from the start."

[The Diamond Sutra commentary is found in *Always Only One*; the Heart Sutra commentary is from the ebook *The Heart of Living*. Dalai Lama's book is *Essence of the Heart Sutra*.]

No Complaints?

Your advisory sentence, "Never let negative thinking gain the upper hand," deserves further contemplation. In its own way, it's negative thinking.

This is followed by another advisory sentence: "Change your thinking, change your life."

And following this, you give the Shakespeare quote: "There is nothing either good or bad, but thinking makes it so."

It is thinking that our thoughts are *either* good or bad, positive or negative, that creates much of our mental anguish; that is, unnecessary suffering.

Why categorize your thoughts as "this" or "that"? Why not merely observe what is *present*—the actual *fact* of what appears on the screen of consciousness—without judgment; with "choiceless awareness"?

Why attempt to change your thinking at all? Why not be present with whatever is present, without wishing or hoping that it will be other than what it is?

In the anecdote which precedes your sentences, the person's "prayer" is: "Thanks for everything. I have no complaints whatsoever."

If, indeed, he now has "no complaints whatsoever," it's because he stopped making judgments about what is "positive" or "negative," and adopted (whether or not he called it this) *choiceless* awareness.

When we truly and *sincerely* say, "Thanks for everything," we mean *everything*—not merely the positive side of the ledger. If we view either side of the ledger as needing to be changed, we're letting "negative thinking gain the upper hand."

Short Take

At the end of life, there is *nothing*. BUT nothing is all there *is*. Now we'll simply know presence *as* presence—because all we then are *is* presence. The body initially became an animate form *in* presence, and presence has been *in* the body. When our body becomes inanimate, it's still in *presence*. And presence *remains* everywhere always. As body-less presence, we'll only know of nothing.

Nothing Person-al

Bear in mind, Ron, that some of the early Sanskrit material was voicing the nondual perspective, *but* not all such material. In fact, Shankara's debates with Brahmins (in which he distilled the essence of Advaita) were centered around the confusions such contradictory doctrines generated.

Much of this same kind of confusion exists in Christianity today, where "worship" is directed toward images, persons such as Mary, or Messengers.

So, you ask, what is one to say about bhakti ("devotion, worship"); or prayer?

Worship can only persist, as Ramana says, "so long as there is a sense of separation." One is only truly *devoted* when one has merged one's "self" into the Absolute. "Then," Ramana says, "*Who* is the worshipper? The answer is: the Self."

Likewise, he says, "There must be an 'I' who prays. If 'God's Will be done,' why pray at all? There is no necessity to let *Him* know your needs: God doesn't require an intermediary. God is *in* all, and works *through* all."

*

If you would like to make God laugh,
tell him your plans.
– Proverb

In Absence of Self-Pity

An Ojai resident, he addressed an attentive audience of forty people, at the Ojai Retreat one mid-May, on the subject of "living on the edge of dying."

In a matter-of-fact tone, punctuated with an enthusiastic chuckle and descriptive gestures, Gordon Farrell buoyantly described how cancer acts as a personal wake-up call.

In the latter months of 1988, his busy career as a commercial photographer in San Francisco had brought him to the brim of financial success. He had energetically kept his nose to the Type-A fast track, resting only five hours a night, seven days a week. "At that time, my favorite song was 'I am a rock; I am an island...'"

He was then in his mid-thirties. Now in his late forties, with close-cropped brown hair, and a beard backed by a dimpled grin, his solid body is that of a former high-school football player.

"I had always been healthy." Then came the day when he touched a hard lump in his abdomen. Stopping by for a cursory check at his doctor's office, he soon found himself in a day-long escalation of pathology tests at the Stanford University medical center. Concluding a CAT scan with biopsies, the diagnosis: cancer in the lymphatic network, which is the body's defensive tackle. And cancer's end run: metastasis in pancreas, lung, bone marrow—and the abdominal tumor. Prognosis: too advanced for surgery, chemotherapy or radiation. Time left in the game: three to six months.

It is rare for oncologists to encounter fourth-stage cancer which has been entirely untreated. Gordon's participation was solicited for a program of experimentation in the interest of medical science. He was informed that he could anticipate a "fifty-fifty chance of survival." When he mused aloud about this "fifty-fifty chance of surviving cancer," he was corrected: "No, no. We mean a fifty-fifty chance of surviving the *experimental program*." Gordon chose to punt. He notes wryly that the experimental program since floundered, and has been discontinued.

Driving home from the research facility, Gordon recalls that he felt no fear, only—to his surprise—a sense of relief. "I no longer had to do all that ambitious stuff anymore."

If there is a reason that he is alive today, it seems to hinge on his first response, which was to squarely face the fact of his impending death; having avoided "denial," he was positioned to radically alter his customary lifestyle.

Retiring to his home state of Oregon, in complete surrender to his present condition, he "began to meditate, in solitude." There might be a period of weeks when he spoke to no one.

Within eighteen months, intense pain preceded spontaneous loss of consciousness, and numerous injurious falls. Gordon learned that if he abandoned resistance to the pain, it could be neutralized; and that if he surrendered to the reality of each moment, discomfort was unlikely to ensue. Such awareness requires attention: each fumble provided a reminder. At one point, the abdominal tumor—which girdles his aortic artery—clenched, provoking a near-fatal experience. "Friends who visited were soon leaving in tears."

He found himself in contact with a parade of people who had either experienced cancer or were knowledgeable about alternative therapies. The touch of each person served to further open his heart, and to replenish his healing energies. "I would not be here, if it were not for these friends."

Four years after moving to Oregon, he returned to California. "I've had no pancreatic pain in nearly four years. The bone marrow pain is gone. The lung cancer has become encapsulated. And though some of the lymph tumors have grown, some have diminished." The abdominal tumor is still present to the touch, and still harnesses the aortic artery.

Though the only day he spent in medical school was his day in the Stanford facility, he says with conviction, "The number one reason why people die from cancer is *fear*." He is not opposed to allopathic treatment: but as a possible *last* resort, not *first*. "Though I have respect for doctors, they treat the symptoms, not the cause."

He adds, "Everyone has cancerous cells in the body, at any point in time." In any case, "every one of us is *terminal*!"

Terminal illness, he observes, "can bring our attention to the present moment." Further, "Pain itself can be a gateway. I've had a lot of experience with it, and I have been *helped* by it. Pain can be the guide to a return to wholeness."

Ending his talk with a discussion with the audience, a 60-year-old woman remarked that although she's had breast cancer, she has rejected mastectomy. "And I want to corroborate what you've said. Cancer has been a powerful teacher for me. Eight years ago, my life became dramatically *better* because of my cancer. And if I have only one more year, I have now learned to live one day at a time!"

Denouement: Prior to the occasion of giving another talk, Gordon wrenched a muscle in his back while riding his horse. Contrary to his better judgment, he resorted to taking pain-killers so that he would not have to cancel the talk. It is this disruption in his alternative-therapy program that he believes caused the abdominal tumor to reinvigorate. He died within a couple of months after that last talk.

Letting Go

You write about your friend Ken's cancer diagnosis, and his assurance that he is "seeking a treatment plan." You add: "I see no point to this...I would not seek to prolong my life. And I remember reading that Krishnamurti did not seek treatment."

True; after it was clear that Krishnamurti had cancer, he accepted only pain relief (morphine) until his death in bed. I have known a number of people who were influenced by Krishnamurti; they have tended to die peacefully.

Krishnamurti did, at one point (after a final meeting with his assistants), decline any further morphine or medication, allowing himself to die.

One of his "followers," whom I knew, ceased all eating and drinking in the hospital, allowing herself to die.

I'd say the attitude is to employ no "heroic measures" to remain alive, retaining the option to hasten one's demise when it is evident that recovery—and "quality of life"—will not be regained.

Considering what you've told me about Ken in the past, my guess is that he will decline radical "life-prolonging" measures, and allow nature to take its course.

Hope-less

On your two observations:

Some people, who don't really understand advaita, speak of teachers who are "advaita" or "neo-advaita." As Tony Parsons has commented, "The term Neo-Advaita is a misnomer."

The bottom line for the nondual teachings, including advaita, is *nothingness*—emptiness, or Void. *Neo* refers to something which has been modified, changed in content. Nothingness is not subject to change; as is, say, colonialism modified into neo-colonialism. In other words, neo-advaita makes no more sense than "neo-nothing."

What the epithet "neo-advaita" is trying to say is that there are different styles which an advaita teacher might employ. Depending on who is being addressed, the emphasis might be purely on the aspect of the Absolute ("there is no doer") or might relate to both the relative and the Absolute ("okay, *you* are the doer—but *who* are 'you'?"). At one point a seeker might declare, "I am That!" At a later point, she might state: "There is no *I*, and there is no *That*." Do we have a *seeker* and a *neo-seeker*?

The most sensible response to the term neo-advaita is to disregard it.

*

You have to bear in mind that for some people, all of this is just entertainment. They've had a long-time interest in this subject; and whenever they find time to read or hear about it, it makes them feel "spiritual."

This kind of person generally enjoys arguing about some of the nuances ("only a vegetarian could be enlightened"), and often holds that only the three persons he can name were ever Self-realized.

So for some, Self-realization is merely a matter for pastime discussion, not a life-changing investigation. This is often because the person doesn't believe that Self-realization is possible for him—*or* for *you*. So, you can't expect that everyone is going to take seriously what it is that you're pointing out.

Deconstruct the Constructor

In answer to your first question, you should note (and ponder) Maharshi's comment in your issue of *Inner Directions*: "There is no such thing as 'realizing' the Self. How is one to real-ize, or 'make real', what is already real?"

From the standpoint of the jnani (enlightened), there is *no one* to whom "enlightenment" pertains; the jnani does not view him/herself as an individual. Where there is *only* That (by whatever name you call it), not any thing can be considered to be individuated (separate from other things).

From the standpoint of the so-called "unenlightened individual," there is some "thing(s)" or condition *apart* from him/her. When this person discovers that they are nothing more than That—and That *only*—the *ideas* of "individual," and an individual's "enlightenment," fall away entirely. Paradoxically, this is what is referred to as "enlightenment"!

So, enlightenment is an illusion, as far as the jnani is concerned. When the ajnani is no longer "in the dark," it is an illusion to him/her also!

Second part of this question:

How to tell "truth" from "illusion"? When you recognize that there is *only That*—*all* things are *That*—"truth" is that, *and* "illusion" is that too! Such distinctions—*all* distinctions—are ultimately meaningless. Even when you fall into deep sleep *tonight*, do you ponder the meaning of truth or illusion? No: they are then nonexistent, as are all other things and their distinctions. The jnani is "asleep" while apparently "awake." He sees *only That*.

Yes (continuing with your queries), you are "beyond desires and their patterns, and the principles that trigger them"—to the extent that you recognize this to be so. "Why should one bother to think about or correct them?": no need to bother—to the extent that you recognize that you are actually "beyond them."

Continuing: if there is no such thing (as the jnani asserts) as truth or illusion, can there be any such thing as karma? Who is the "individual" that presumes that some "one" or some "thing" somewhere is evaluating and recording our actions and movements? *All* is *That*: *you* are That, what "you" *do* is That. In your deepest sleep, there is no identifiable "you"; if that is your condition in deep sleep, will it be otherwise in death? So then, to whom is the history of "your" activities—good or bad—to be *attached*?

Recognize that when the contents of your consciousness are stripped away (or disappear as in deep sleep), only one condition remains: *pure* awareness. That is the core of "who" or "what" you are. It is unchanging. All else is changing.

All that you identify as *you* will evaporate at some point: at death...or possibly before. Frame all your questions from the standpoint of an awareness that has dissolved into That, into the condition that is "experienced" in the amnesia of deep sleep. Consider each time: what is the significance of this question, when there exists no separate I to ask it?

Words, to the Wise

One of the problems with the word "spirit"—in addition to its association with ghostly *entities*—is that it is definitionally "regarded as separate from matter."

Where one uses the word spirit (which I think it best to avoid) as an alternate to Omnipresence (or Absolute, That, etc.), it must be made clear that, in its all-pervasiveness, it is not separate from *any* thing.

This is why "soul" is an even more troublesome word: "An *entity* regarded as being *part* of a *person*, thought of as separate from the body." Thus all of the theological references to "your" soul, "my" soul, the "sinner's" soul, the "redeemed" soul, et al—the soul which is presumed to transmigrate (individually) to Heaven. This has no relevance at all to that which is characterized as utterly formless, permeating infinitely and eternally, "nowhere that it's *not*."

Why resort to ambiguously confusing terms when clearer secular terms are available?

What's Possible?

Spiritual teachers sometimes speak of the "I don't know" mind. Sometimes they also speak of the "empty mind."

The I-don't-know mind doesn't refer to a condition where one has no interest in arriving at the Truth of the nature of our existence. Whereas one might respond to the classical question "Who am I?" with the initial acknowledgement "I don't know," *this* I-don't-know is not meant to imply "and I have no inclination to find out" Or, "I don't believe that it's possible for *anyone* to know."

The I-don't-know mind, that's suggested, is an *open* mind, a mind which is without preconceptions as to what might be discovered in the inquiry pertaining to "who am I?" In this sense, it is related to what is spoken of as an "empty mind," a mind which is open to the discovery of a truth which cannot be conceptualized. Suzuki Roshi called this a "beginner's" mind; noting that, for a beginner in any endeavor, the possibilities are endless, but for the "expert" the possibilities are closed to a limited number.

An empty mind is both the beginning point and the ending point of the spiritual inquiry. The I-don't-know mind can be misinterpreted to be simply the *end*, the close of the spiritual discussion.

Wholly-ness

A part can never be anything—even though given a new identity—but a fragment of a shattered whole. The meaning of *part* is "a portion of the whole." Even a "complete" portion is only an incomplete part of wholeness.

If we were to shatter a vase and reassemble it, even though all of its parts were present, we would normally say that the vase had lost its wholeness. A vase which is truly whole contains all elements, including its wholeness.

In a sense, a universe contains all elements, and no parts are in conflict, because there are no 'parts' to be found.

It is the nature of the human mind to separate everything into parts. Every "thing" in the universe *is* the thing, or fragment or shard, that it is, because the mind of man has extracted "objects" from wholeness and has named them as such. A *thing*, if we refer to its meaning, is "that which is distinguished to be a specific entity." And it is the mind of man which does the distinguishing (L.: "pick apart", differentiate), through the process of thought.

And so it is the mind of man, his thought, which seizes ahold of a fragment of the actuality of the whole universe; and he identifies or names it as a separate, existing entity. This can be a convenience. Say, a baby is born at home. The father calls to report to the mother's doctor. "Is the baby okay?" the doctor asks. By *baby*, he means this newly born "body." "Yes, the body is whole," the father replies. By *body*, he means every portion of the whole baby: arms, legs, head, eyes, toes, etc. "But," the father continues, "there is a strange spot on the body." The doctor says, "Oh, where is the spot? What *part* of the body?" But the body has no *parts*, in that there is not anything separate from it, nothing that could be handed over "in sale." Yet the father and the doctor fracture the wholeness of the meaning of *body* (or *baby*) by agreeing to distinguish, as a specific entity or thing, that which has utterly no independence from the condition of wholeness. "The chest," replies the father. "It's a blemish," he adds, further removing the spot from what might otherwise be an unbroken wholeness.

Even the cosmos—though its identification by a word reduces it to a thing—is not a part, since it represents all that exists, or is: the whole of actuality, in as broad of a linear perspective as the imagination of man can conceive it. Yet we (agree to) say that a 'part' of this cosmos is *mankind*; and a part of mankind is *me*.

This is a convenient artifice, to the *practical* extent to which I wish to ignore the wholeness of the universe. But when, through customary usage, I lose awareness of the whole because of my chronic concentration on the 'parts', I have lost what is *essential* (L: be-ing.). Another word which derives from the same root as *whole* is "health," which is "absence of dis-order."

A partial, or partisan view, is a conflicting view (in that there can be no conflict in something which has no opposing parts). To the extent to which you and I understand, thus agree upon, the order or nature of things, there will not be opposition and conflict. But where divisive thinking (however un-conscious) is at work—whether among one mind or more—there will be proportionate conflict, strife or strain.

For some, who have barely recognized the truth of this, there is the strain or conflict of endeavoring to *restore* to wholeness that which has never—except by determination—been severed from the start. And so the *realization* of wholeness is: "the condition which cannot in actuality be divided or differentiated in any meaningful or absolute way."

This would even mean, by extenuation, that the baby's blemish is not something which ought to be regarded as something un-wholesome in the universe.

Wholeness is not something that has to be contrived or engineered. It is present naturally.

But this will not normally be admitted. This indivisibility can be—and usually is—ignored by the mind which has been conditioned to habitually and chronically focus on "parts."

In our concentration on the world of the material, we thoroughly ignore the essential nature of existence: not anything is important *in itself.* The meaning of universality is that not anything assumes precedence over anything else. Put another way, no *part* of existence can have more meaning than the *whole* of existence, nor any other 'part.'

Ignoring inherent wholeness by focusing on supposedly independent parts, we strive to glue the shards together and to restore wholeness. Wholeness, universality, indivisibility need not be restored: it has never, for a moment, been absent. But it is constantly being "under-looked."

And, viewing only division wherever he looks, man is consequently in constant conflict—with "self" and "other." Thus, he is continually in search of wholeness *because* he neglects to see it in himself, and in others.

Naked Awareness

For about a year, while between permanent homes some years ago, I lived at a nudist resort near San Diego. Folks, that I talked to there, seemed convinced that the population of nudists was steadily increasing. I reflected on the soaring increase in sheer human numbers, and it occurred to me that any increase in the nudist population probably only reflected a general population increase.

Acquaintances sometimes remark to me that the attraction to the nondual teachings appears to be increasing at a surprising rate. Earlier on, this seemed to me to be a corollary to the increase in the nudist population. But, more recently, I've considered it differently.

In one-on-one discussions with scores of people each of the past few years, I've noticed that virtually all of these "seekers" have much in common. Most all have acquainted themselves with a wide variety of spiritual teachings and disciplines. Most all have been involved in some sort of "practice"-oriented tradition, various schools of meditation primarily among them.

Partly due to such books as Alan Watts' *Way of Zen*, there was a notable enthusiastic interest in Buddhism beginning in the Sixties. Many Zen roshis were invited over from Japan to establish zendos in the various parts of the U.S., such as Suzuki Roshi who headed the San Francisco Zen Center.

The so-called sudden enlightenment school of Soto Zen seems to have been more attractive than Rinzai Zen with its koan stepping-stones. Soto Zen masters stressed Zazen, sitting meditation.

One prominent nonduality teacher today, Adyashanti (Steve Gray) has had experience with Zazen (as have I). If Buddhism was purely in the business of enlightenment, he has observed, it would be bankrupt by now.

There are men and women who've been diligently pursuing their meditation (or other) practice for twenty, thirty, even fifty years to date, who will tell you that they are still not Self-realized. An all-too-common email lies next to me on my desk: "I have practiced (Buddhist) meditation, and studied in many traditions. However, I have not been able to realize my essential nature. What is the practice that allowed you to realize your nondual state, in a permanent way?" A recent issue of a Theravada quarterly provoked despairing letters-to-the-editor concerning this very matter.

What I have described in the preceding paragraph is to me the answer to why there is a burgeoning interest in Advaita. The fundament of this teaching is that what you are seeking is actually inescapable, and you need merely recognize that fact. Your "essential nature" *must* be here, now. Any, and every, practice can only focus your attention on a desired future event, piping your awareness away from the Presence that is always everywhere—whether you are sitting thoughtless on a cushion, or *not*.

Mixed Up

The greatest error one can make in attempting to understand nonduality is to expect to "have it both ways"; i.e., to posit both the dualistic perspective and the nondualistic perspective in the same proposition.

For instance, if you ask: As the Absolute, how am I to relate to others?

As the Absolute, or from the perception of Oneness, there are no "others."

One can only ponder one's relationship, to others, where there is "me" and the not-me; or "me" and the "other" (or others) than me.

From the standpoint of the Absolute, there are no "relationships," such as *my* relationship to *others*. There are no "two (or more) things" in nonduality.

So the proposition, mentioned above, is a non-sequitur.

One can only legitimately ask: How do I (1) relate to others (2)? (Duality.)

Or: Do others—or even I—*exist*, apart from the Absolute? (If not, there can *be* no *relationship*.)

Grace is....

Ramana Maharshi was sometimes asked "Is Self-realization a matter of grace, a gift that is allotted to some worthy few?"

Ramana responded, "It is grace that you are *inquiring*, that you are seeking to merge with ultimate Reality."

You now are graced with this inquiry into the nature of universal truth.

When you light a flame to one corner of this page, consummation takes place of its own accord. Allow the spark of your attraction to Self-realization to ignite an all-encompassing flame.

*

"For *everyone*, it (awakening) is undoubtedly possible."
–Ramana

Cut to the Chase

Your latest letter was written over five days, you said. I'm required to be more brief.

There are a couple of aspects of the nondual realization which seem to be discovered only with the greatest difficulty, by most everyone.

The first is that the revelation, of the empty truth, is discovered to be unimpeded by time. Why? Because the seeker *is* that which is *sought*. There is nowhere you need to go, and *nothing you need to do* in order to be *connected* to that which is the *source* of all that is. This omnipresent actuality, this unbroken Presence, is so thoroughly immersed *in* everything that it *is* everything. Therefore you—despite who you purport to be—are That. *Being* That, you will not, at any *other* time, be *nearer* to That. *Whether or not* you acknowledge your "true nature," you are That. So, being That *this very moment*, time is irrelevant. You need not, if you awaken to the fact, occupy yourself with a pursuit for the presence of the limitless actuality any longer: you cannot even *escape* That!

The second matter is a recognition which is implicitly entwined with the first.

Described as being *"nowhere* that it is *not,"* it is effectually the actual essence of all that is. All formulated identities (each of which is merely a differentiated thought) are superficial, synthetic. No matter what we point to, its fundamental identity is reduced to *That*. Not anything comes into existence *apart* from infinite Presence, so the identity of all forms is subsumed in the formless Presence out of which they arise. Your assumed identity disappears, dissolves, when the true nature of this totality is recognized. *Whether or not* you acknowledge this fundamental truth, "you" do not *exist* as a separate, independent entity.

Nor does—and this is the key element—any "thing" *else* as a *separately*-identifiable reality. Each and every word-distinction falls into the maw, the void, of the formless totality. By whatever name we want to call that formless void, even *that name* is *meaningless*. What *definition*, for example, can you put into the word "God" when there is *nothing but* God? With nothing whatsoever that can stand in contrast, why even the need for such a word, a distinction ("distinct *from*"), as God—or any other title or designation: such as Void, Presence, That, Oneness, etc., etc.?

The essence of the nondual realization, as Zen puts it, is that "there is not *any thing* on which to stand." *Nor anyone* to stand upon it. *Even the Void* disappears when it is realized that no one ultimately exists to recognize the void!

When there is *not anything but God*, WHO is to make reference to God?

If such reference were to be made, only *God* could remain to make the reference.

You are *That* which *refers* to That. You are That in recognition of its Self.

Every (so-called) small-s self *is* the capital-S Self—including *your* self.

When you awaken to the fact that you *are* That, what is left of the "struggle" to find, or connect with God?

How could anyone or anything be apart from That which is *defined* as illimitable?

This is the basic, *vital issue*. When it becomes clear that the "person" you consider yourself to be is a false identification, all of "your" past becomes irrelevant. All of your acquired knowledge is rendered useless. Matters that have to do with "my ego" are immediately resolved. Spiritual experiences, passing phenomenon, even "surrender" and "transcendence" no longer have any meaning at all.

Who transcends, when there is no one apart from anything to begin with?

What could one ultimately surrender to, when that which surrenders *is* what it surrenders *to*?

It is possible to cut to the chase, and to be finished with every spiritual teaching, by opening to the *basic* truth the teachers are offering: the "you" that you want to believe exists, *really* exists only as a self-imposed fantasy. In present awareness, it is possible to snap out of this fantasy.

A Glimpse of Merging

The enlightenment of each sage has followed a different process: no two alike. However, when you read the biographies of each of these enlightened sages, you notice that they collectively had one thing in common: the profundity of enlightenment is a life-changing development. The bottom line, in these recorded lives, is that there was a radical change between the pre-enlightenment life style and the life's consequent course.

If you listen to electronic recordings of "spiritual" workshops, satsanga, retreats etc., you will frequently hear this comment from attendees: "I had a glimpse of the ultimate state once, but it has disappeared." The reason for this is simple: the commentator has not transcended the subject/object perspective; there has been a "glimpse" to a "glimpser"; there was a persistent "I" in relation to a "spiritual experience." In other words, the participant hasn't fundamentally understood and transcended the perspective which we call dualism. The seeker's presumption was that "I can have an experience of the One." And so there is an "I" on the one hand, and "the One" on the other hand.

Every "experience" is impermanent; it occurs within the time frame of an "experiencer." As the time–bound experience concludes, the experiencer's I-consciousness recurs. There remains the "I" with its "glimpse."

With the "I" remaining central to one's perception, there will be no radical change in one's self-centered life matrix. Only when this I-centered perspective has *irretrievably* dissolved will there be the true groundswell of matrix-breaking enlightenment.

Clearly, it is not uncommon for retreat-weekend "spiritual" participants to have an experience of a "glimpse" of "merging." But when they come away from that "training" with the dualistic I/It mindset still *unconsciously* in place, there will be no permanent, substantial realization of the perspective known as nonduality—a *permanent*, thorough, *annihilating* change of the "experiencer" perception.

After Enlightenment, What?

One may come to a realization of one's true identity, that sense of not-twoness that has been spoken of by (among others) Buddha, Jesus, Ramana or Krishnamurti. Such an awakening will thenceforth shape the remainder of one's entire life. It will have a profound impact upon what one considers to be "right livelihood," or one's relationship to "family." But one will discover—once again—that there is no *external* "authority" to whom one can turn for guidance.

Buddha did not know firsthand the life of the breadwinner. Even though, as a prince, he deserted his father's royal estate, the knowledge that he would be welcomed upon return to his comfortable home could not have been but a solace to him. And while, as a young man, he fathered a child, he had abandoned such familial responsibilities thereafter.

Jesus, during the eighteen unaccounted years said to begin with his teens, may—being the son of a carpenter—have been a laborer. And it is possible that he may, as well, have been a husband or parent during this period. However, recent historical conjecture suggests that those "missing" years might have been spent wandering abroad in India, where he adopted his radical spirituality. It is possible too that he never knew the life of a workingman or of a householder.

Ramana Maharshi left home, upon illumination, at about age 16, and was evidently chaste, neither a family man nor a worker, throughout his long lifetime.

Krishnamurti, similar in tradition to the Tibetan lamas, was designated for his role while still a dependent youngster, and also was neither a wage earner nor a spouse for his long lifetime.

Furthermore, the first three of these men lived in a climate where one could (as each had done) sleep out of doors under a tree; and in a culture where one *could* (as each had done) depend on sympathetic passersby for one's food. And there is evidence that any of these sages could have returned to their parents' home, had they chosen.

The daily dilemmas which confront a truthseeker in the colder climate where food and shelter are available only for cash, credit or food stamps; where any but the most menial jobs require an unblemished résumé; where one may be legally obligated and committed to family responsibilities— or, on the other hand, may have no family whom one may depend upon...these challenges can be instructive in that they can be responded to only moment by moment, day by day, bereft of the authority of the past, and consistent only with one's attunement to the simple ramifications of wholeness.

*

> "Beware of all enterprises that
> require new clothes."
> – Emerson

An Open Secret

There is an essential point which I think you may be poised to discover for yourself; the Dalai Lama speaks of a secret "which lies hidden and obscured by conceptual thinking." A lama would have penetrated this secret, so obviously it would be a perception which eludes our normal, conceptual cognitive framework.

The Dalai Lama has spoken of two aspects of awareness, one being "natural" or "inherent" to us (for which he uses the Dzochen term, rigpa), the other being an (adopted) awareness that is secondary, the result of our conditioning, or learning.

This latter (which he refers to as gross consciousness) is—for most people—*normative* awareness, which is basically superimposed on our *natural* awareness (rigpa).

Our selective, menial consciousness ("gross" or "relative") arises within, as it were, our visceral and universal consciousness (that which animates our body regardless of our individual conditioning).

To narrow down the raft of terms, let us say that the selective, analytic aspect is "relative," and the aspect which naturally is clear of relative concerns and conceptualized objects is our innate, universal or "absolute" (nonobjective, undifferentiated) condition, or awareness, or "mind."

To avoid potential abstractions, let's say that the *relative* aspect of awareness, or "thought," focuses attention on mundane matters, such as "what should be," "what could be," "what will be," "what has been," etc. The universal aspect of awareness is attentive always to "what is."

One of the *elements*, in its awareness of what is, is the ("internal") activity of the constantly preoccupied, relative mind: the relative mind arrives at a conclusion or decision; the universal awareness is "aware of," in observance of (like an impartial witness), one more phenomenal event, or thought.

The nature of the relative mind, being an individual-ized artifact, is that it is fragmentary. Due to the necessary limitations within which its acquired and accumulated knowledge operates, it is—from the wholistic standpoint—a sea of confusion. In occasional moments of inactivity, when the restless waves momentarily subside, the truer aspect of our awareness recognizes this confusion. Feeling (or noticing) a sense of contrast in our consciousness, we intuitively long for a deeper expression of the imperturbable aspect of our nature.

In consequence, we might find ourselves consciously studying what is written about Dzochen, or one of the other forms of illumination.

As beginning *students*, habituated by our comparative and objectifying mind, we will *presume* that a lama has substituted or replaced the relative mind with thoughtless awareness. From the bias of our either-or perspective, we will endeavor to discredit our relative (limited) thoughts and establish in their place "impartial" thoughts. In the context in which we're speaking, we will endeavor to transact a shift from the mind which would *not* be characterized as rigpa, to the condition which we suppose *would* be characterizable as rigpa.

The secret, we eventually come to learn, is that no such effort is necessary: there is not anything which needs to be replaced. Rigpa is a matter of recognition: recognizing that undesired mentation is a phenomenon of the *same* mind which quietly observes it with no reaction (as rigpa).

The undesired mentation occurs in a condition of awareness which is operating in relative terms: there is an "object"— undesirable manifestation—and a subject: to whom this particular manifestation is undesirable. To our "unborn mind"—that which existed prior to the self—there *is* no discernible subject (I) nor object (mind, thought, etc.); in *this* awareness, there is neither this or that; neither "desirable" or "undesirable."

The innate, unconditioned awareness dispassionately observes the phenomenal activity of the analytical, superficial mind. Yet it is in no way disconnected from, or apart from, that...in the same way that your left hand is not disconnected from your right hand.

To attempt to eradicate, or ameliorate, the activity of your relative mind—whether conceived of as "good" or "bad"— is as un-necessary as a bilateral lobe removal in your brain.

The relative aspect of awareness and the witnessing aspect are like two facets of a gemstone, each facet needing no justification.

Rigpa is to recognize what is, "internally" and "externally," and to let it be as it is. And among that which is, is the "undesirable" activity which appears to occur within our individual psyche. Merely see it for what it is—impermenant phenomenon—and let it go.

Then rigpa is *your* secret.

Notice that, as the Dalai Lama states, in the "natural" [unborn, "primordial"] condition of the mind "there is no objectivity [subject as opposed to object] involved....

> "You are not preoccupied by what arises in the mind ['good' or 'bad'], nor does it cause you any distress.... You do not employ...discursive [analytical; e.g. 'this is okay,' 'this is not rigpa'] thoughts....

> "(What) we are talking about is an *extra*-ordinary quality of awareness [not our normative, perfunctory condition]..."

This extra-ordinary quality, of rigpa, is that there is

> "...no inner and no outer [relative notions], nothing like 'this' or 'that' [rigpa; not rigpa], nothing to be experienced by something experiencing it ['*I* am experiencing rigpa'; or 'I am not experiencing rigpa'], and no duality of subject and object whatsoever [*me* as opposed to—or separate from—my relative, *or* witnessing, awareness]."

The fact of the matter is that to make such distinctions as indicated above is to operate in (or from) relative awareness, the form of consciousness which Eastern mystics refer to as illusional—not reflecting our true, fundamental nature. The mind which distinguishes "good" from "bad" is the mind which generates our suffering; *maya* (illusion) is the seed of *dukha* (suffering). Illusion is not a product of *witnessing* awareness; it is a product of "gross consciousness"—separative, relativistic cognition: "dualistic thinking."

But, dualistic awareness has its (particularizing) function; non-dualistic has its (non-particularizing) function: *both* are awareness. To be immersed in one condition in exclusion to the other is to be in a state of distraction from our fundamental human potential.

When Namkhai Norbu says, "stay present in this recognition without getting distracted," one would normally interpret this in the customary (separative) way: "Keep your understanding of rigpa forever present in your awareness lest gross consciousness interdict." Could it be that such a preoccupation would be the very *distraction* which he is alluding to? Might it not be that "this recognition" is that rigpa is the Tibetan equivalent of choiceless awareness? The message, in whatever language, is to observe whatever arises *as it is*—good, bad, or otherwise—and not be distracted with ideas about how manifestations ought to *ideally* occur: "then all impurities dissolve [automatically, under such circumstances, without effort on your part]; this is the [secret] essence of the path."

Could it be, when the Dalai Lama comments, "The most difficult task is to differentiate between ordinary mind and rigpa," that he himself—operating on the undifferentiating continuum—does not burden himself with this difficult task, because he no longer concerns himself with *this* "mind" and *that* "rigpa"?

"Only when the mind is not fragmented," says Krishnamurti, "what you see in totality is the truth."

When the mind is fragmented, it can perceive only *either* and *or*. When the mind is whole, *"either"* and *"or"* are one and the same truth.

Our native awareness, being unbroken, encompasses all that is—including the fragmented. To move 'from' a fragmented mind 'to' an un-fragmented mind is merely to recognize that the former is an extension, a subject, of the latter—not removed in space or time. In the enlightened mind, one condition is not "preferred" over another, because both are understood to be inseparable elements of the one, same reality—which has no identifiable qualities, either good or bad.

Non-conceptual Seeing

An "intellectual seeing," as you put it, is a matter of understanding that I and the Absolute are one.

The "experiential seeing," that you speak of, is the disappearance of the subtle duality in which two (supposedly "different") concepts are "united."

You need to first recognize that the 'I' is a (separative) concept. Then you need to understand that the 'I,' which is unreal, seeks to complete itself by the addition of (unification with) the Absolute: in this context, we have a concept-ion of the Absolute as some thing we could possibly be apart from, in the first place (thus, the "uniting").

When you comprehend what the enlightened masters have said—you ARE what you seek; or, the observer IS the observed—the I "disappears," *and* the I's (false) conception of the "other" dissolves; with what remains, there are no ideas about seeking, anything.

It's alright to say, "there is an individual here"; from the relative, dualistic standpoint, that would appear to be so.

But if, as you say, "there can be no separation," then in truth there can be no such reality as "individuals."

It is the INDIVIDUAL who is seeking unity; the Absolute condition, itself, IS one of no separation: not two, not even one (nothing to conceive, or conceive being apart from).

At present, you are insisting, at least by way of concept, that there is a separate YOU (this is the "seeker"). When it's thoroughly taken seriously that there can in actuality be no such things as a separate you, what "is left" is the

Absolute condition. And, it is impossible to unite with this, because it's already always ever-present. If you weren't conceiving otherwise, you'd know that you can't come into union with that which no one has ever been apart from.

Wee Little Drops

Consciousness is all there is, say the sages.

As an analogy, let us think of consciousness as the ocean. Then a wave, as a manifestation of the ocean, is merely an extension of that consciousness. As the wave crests, and droplets of water are spewed, the droplets of water are simply an extension of the wave. These droplets of water are particles of the ocean of consciousness.

Suzuki Roshi utilized the occasion of a visit to a waterfall to extend the analogy. Extrapolating from his presentation, let us consider as "consciousness" the body of water which rushes toward the precipice; it strikes a rock along the topmost rim of the waterfall and splashes into droplets which plummet parallel to the cliffside.

As consciousness, let us say that a droplet is suddenly conscious of its individuation or separation from the source, having suddenly been born into its condition of freefall. It looks to its left at another drop of water (a "different," slightly larger drop), mutually created at about the same moment and accompanying it on the same downward course.

"Hey, look at me!" shouts the drop, above the din of the roaring cataract. "I'm independent—an individual!"

"Me too!" exults the other drop.

Each now has, for the time being, an identification: Big Drop as an object of consciousness of Little Drop; and Little Drop, objectified through the consciousness of the Big Drop.

Had the primary source of consciousness—the body of water—not broken apart or manifested as particles, it could be conscious of nothing apart from itself: a closed loop. My awareness of being "me" (the Little Drop) is a reflection of my awareness of "you" (the Big Drop), and vice versa.

Another particle of water-source is falling alongside of them—composed of algae.

"What's that?" says the Little Drop.

"I dunno," says the Big Drop; "but it ain't *us*. It appears to be apart from consciousness!"

Their journey downward continues, as time passes. Had they not been individuated from the body of water, there would be no "time" as an object of their consciousness; moving indivisibly throughout a unitary body, there would be no special or separate "events" (such as birth) by which to benchmark a measure for time.

So, too, for the separation of distance or "space"; perspectives which are relative to their apparent individuation would be unapparent, indivisible within the body of water.

Their journey suddenly ends, as their individuation dies on the mossy rocks at the foot of the waterfall, and they resume their corporeal identity with their source.

When sages of centuries past said that consciousness is all there is, they were merely presaging what science is discovering today.

A drop of water, a scientist would say, is a cohesion of molecules of hydrogen and oxygen; a slightly different cohesion of these molecules, with nitrogen added, would be described as air.

Molecules are an aggregation of atoms, and atoms are composed of subatomic particles. Each particle, such as an electron, is entirely interchangeable with any other electron in the universe; in this way, they are indistinguishable. It has been said, for example, that there is one electron manifesting in numerous locations throughout the cosmos. Likewise is true for the other subatomic particles.

The Little Drop, even though there are fewer particles in it, is no different than the Big Drop; they are essentially one and the same thing.

Such particles are the substance, the nature, of matter. Everything that exists is composed of one arrangement or another of these universally-present particles.

These particles are not in isolation from each other; if isolated, they are without function, moribund; we could say 'virtual'.

What we call "empty space" is anything but empty. And what appears to be algae, rock, sky, sun, water, etc., are an interconnected network of mutually-interpenetrating subatomic particles. The appearance of all these separate forms is a manifestation of the underlying substrate which is the originating source. These manifestations, their decay and reabsorption—what we call the "life and death" of things—follow a cohesive, intelligent regimen. However chaotic, it has unfailingly persisted.

This intelligence is not apart from the things which exist, any more than a process could be apart from its product, or a product isolated from its process.

This intelligence is no different in essence than that which it manifests *as*. Like a single intelligent electron which operates consistently, in its intelligent electron-fashion wherever it is individually observed in the universe, this intelligence breaks itself apart and reassimilates itself in all parts of the universe at all times, simultaneously.

This phenomenal scale of super-human, inexplicable and mysterious intelligence is what we have traditionally come to call "God." It is what the sages refer to as Consciousness; "Consciousness is all there is."

Examine, consequently, your "relationship" (or the relationship of anything) to God, to that which is Absolute.

When the proposal of the sages is clearly understood, it is "God" who is writing this monograph, and it is also "God" who is at this moment reading it. Put another way, consciousness is writing this, consciousness is reading this; both expressions of the intelligence which "creates," or governs, anything that exists.

An interesting consequence of this understanding unfolds. Any activity which an electron engages in is a manifestation of the "Supreme Being" —it is doing what it is doing because, in the overall development of things, that is what it ought to be doing; some other things will, somehow, be dependent upon what it is doing.

I am compelled to write this monograph (I considered doing other things). You are compelled to read it (you considered doing other things). This monograph did not rely on my intention to write it, on this beautiful day to be out for a walk. My writing it is, fundamentally, consciousness (the Absolute) doing what it does. And if I did not write it, *that* would be consciousness doing what it does, too.

If you have read this and you reflect on the Absolute (consciousness), *that* is the Absolute doing what it does. If you do otherwise—no matter what you do—that is *also* the Absolute doing what it does.

If you understand your "relationship" with the Absolute, *that* is what the Absolute (or "Consciousness") does. If you don't perceive your identity in the Absolute, that, too, is what the Absolute does.

When the sages simply say, "Consciousness is all there is," they do not qualify it with "right consciousness" or "wrong consciousness."

Psychic Phenomena

H.W.L. Poonja, who died in 1997, was a teacher of nonduality in India, known as Poonjaji or "Papaji." When he was still a spiritual seeker, he went to see Ramana Maharshi. Poonja said that he was adept at psychic experiences, and sought to find out from Ramana if that had relevance to the condition of enlightenment. Ramana asked: Is your supernormal experience present right now?

No, Poonja said. Ramana told him: What I experience does not come and go.

Understanding this, Poonja ceased to cultivate psychic abilities. He focused his attention instead on the teachings of nonduality, and became somewhat of a successor to Ramana (who died in 1950).

Study what the spiritual masters have advised concerning this matter. Ramana said psychic experiences, or even powers, are "mere phenomena...only transient...not worth striving for...apt to prove a hindrance to enlightenment...(subjects) will likely lose their way."

Specifically, he is quoted as saying "there is no wisdom in the one (cultivating) them. (Psychic powers) are not worthy of any thought. Self-realization alone is to be aimed at and gained."

The wisest person takes this view: the foremost priority is Self-realization. *If* psychic experiences then manifest, that would be a by-product. There is a possibility that such an occurrence can happen—but not the other way around. Again, research what the enlightened masters have said about this.

The Rush

On this Sunday afternoon, a handful of parishioners warm the pews in the North Austin Church of God. Erected on the lawn outside the church is, for some reason, a satellite disk. There is a chain-link fence around the disk, topped with barbed wire.

Somewhere across the highway from the church, is the Oasis, a typical porn shop. Near the novelty display case and cash register is a large cardboard notice, written with black marker: "Popper ½-Price Sale." All the stock must be sold, it notes, because four days from today (which will be two days after Valentine's Day) the sale of poppers will be illegal in Texas. Lined up on a shelf nearby are rows of small containers, with brand names such as "Rush." When inhaled, the chemicals zap the brain's senses with a brief but instant high—a boot used sometimes at the moment of sexual climax. To provide legitimacy, the chemicals are mixed with a fragrance and the cartridge is sold as an "aroma inhaler."

A man in his forties, with curly hair and curly beard, has asked the clerk for five poppers of a particular brand. Restless, he finds it difficult to stand still while waiting. The clerk, who might be a student at the University of Texas downtown, starts to ring up the sale, but pauses:

"Sure that'll be enough? You know, these are gonna be illegal after the 16th."

The man toys with his wallet. "I'm sure gonna hate to have to go over the border to get 'em."

The clerk drapes a finger on the sign. "And they're half-price now."

"I wonder how long they keep? Yeah, shit, you better give me five more. Maybe that'll last me until I have to go outta the country to get 'em again." He adds with a hollow chuckle, gazing at the ten containers, "If I live that long."

Causation

It was stated in print recently that bone marrow is now known to produce two and a half million new cells per second(!). Perhaps this is an average of, say, two million this second and three million the next second: either way, whether the count is averaged or constant, it prompts reflection.

Where is the counting taking place, in the body, that keeps the cell figure consistently at 2½ million/second? How is 2½ million of anything to be accurately counted each second, hour after hour, day after day?

Even assuming that this volume is allotted according to mass, rather than number, is it the "brain" of the bone marrow which allots and monitors the needed mass? Does the cerebral cortex of the body attend to this particular detail?

In other words, is intelligent direction imposed on this phenomenon from "outside," or is the intelligent direction "internal," inherent to the phenomenon itself? One could say that the cells appear only when the conditions are right; but this would also suggest that the conditions are right only when the cells appear. Does the situation arise due to the presence of intelligence; or does intelligence arise simultaneously with any situation which it involves? Can intelligence be a "cause"? Is it "caused"?

"...Including Me"

I understand that the very nature of the Absolute must mean that everything is That, including me. It could not possibly be otherwise; otherwise the Absolute would be something less than absolute. So the world which I am experiencing is not a world of separate forms, but a world which just appears as separate forms. And yet even after I contemplate this, and understand that it must be the case, there is the continued perception of separation. There is no shift in perspective that gives a first-hand experience of this being the truth/reality. My moment-by-moment experience remains one of separation.

If the illusion is seen as an illusion, then why does it not end immediately?

Your query is well-stated. It is perhaps *the* most prominent of the quandaries posed. Every explanation, or response (a roshi pounds his staff on the floor) is directed to it. All of my books speak directly to it.

"Everything is that, including me." If it's *truly* "understood," it's recognized that anything "you" say, do, or think is That doing what is done. As the Vedas say, "*You* are not the doer." So, to *whom* is any "continued sense of separation" occurring? To *whom* would a "shift in perspective"— or *lack* of it—be perceived? By *whom* is an "illusion" seen— or conceived?

The concluding sentence in the main paragraph begins "My." But it's been asserted that the "me" is *That*. To have it both ways—*That*, as a premise / *me*, as a perspective—is duality.

Is it "the world which *I* am experiencing," or is the world *That*, and the experiencing (by the experienc*er*) *That*?

"The very nature of the Absolute must be that EVERYTHING is That." Absolutely so. If you're being absolutely consistent, and not identifying as *me* one moment and *That* in the next, there will be not two but *one*: then you have eradicated what "appears as separate forms."

So, if the "me" is seen through (as a separate form, leaving the Absolute which is without form) to whom will there be a "shift in perspective"? When there's a recognition that both "shifts" and "no shifts" (or any other conceivable dualistic distinctions) are included in the *everything* which is That, this is what is known as Realization.

Duality is the "illusion." That there is a *me* who would be united with *That* is duality.

Nonduality is the realization "there are *no* two things" in actual truth, despite the *appearance* of "separate forms." Those *appearances*, too, are That!

The sense of "separation" is also an appearance.

"Contemplate this...it must be the case."

Disengage Every Concept

The Ribhu Gita, like others in that genre, is ostensibly an exemplification of an enlightened spiritual teacher (Ribhu) transmitting the nondual precepts to a seasoned aspirant (Nidhaga Rishi) in nearly two thousand verses, or brief paragraphs.*

Presumably, a *rishi* ("seer") would already have a basic grasp of the simple principles of advaita (nonduality), but not yet have intuited the essential connections which underlie complete Self-realization.

The sage Ramana Maharshi sometimes quoted the Ribhu Gita, and encouraged adepts to read it.

Selections highlighting the key points (about a hundred verses) were ably translated into modern English, around thirty years ago, by Prof. N.R. Krishnamoorthi Aiyer for publication by Ramana's ashram in south India.

Such ancient writings are usually somewhat random and repetitive, so they're best understood by following a progressive ordering of the content, as I've done in the commentary below. For brevity, the quotations I've selected have been mostly paraphrased. And all words in parentheses are for clarification.

The Ribhu Gita asserts that Self-realization (a.k.a. enlightenment) "is possible only for those intent on knowing the Self, and not for those who are indifferent."

* Ed. note: see also Robert's commentary on the Ashtavakra Gita in *Always—Only—One.*

The *Self* is a time-honored word for ultimate reality, also sometimes called the Absolute; the timeless, eternal omnipresent beingness ("fundamental, or essential, nature"). In other words, it is the "self" of every existent (or nonexistent) thing, whether animate or inanimate, visible, or invisible. Some would call the Self by other names, such as "God."

Knowing It does not merely mean assuming or believing there is such a thing, but knowing it as you "know" of the "reality" of your own self—your awareness or apprehension of your existence.

Lack (of such awareness), or "indifference in regard to the truth about one's self, is the storehouse of trouble—all sorts of illusions and worry," states the Gita. "Enquire 'what is this world, what is the reality behind all this?'"

And the Gita gives us a major clue as to how to reveal the truth: "Relentlessly pursue until all *conceptual forms merge and disappear.*"

The Gita also states the truth we will discover as a consequence. "Simply put, everything exists always as the Self only."

In an "intellectual" understanding of this statement, one notices the part about everything that exists *being—is—* the divine, or the Self. But the point that is *overlooked* is that "everything" *includes* "me"!

Refer back to the key assertion of this venerated Gita: Everything, always, is *only* the Self. That means, from the standpoint of identity —exist-ence—there are not two (or more) "things": there is One thing, without any differentiation in it. Therefore, "you" are included in that One, *along with* everything "else." The *meaning* of nonduality is "not two"; and so, no "you," no "other than you."

So, from this Absolute standpoint, there is no *separate* "I": what we have known as the I must be only the Self, the ever-present indivisible Ultimate Reality. As the Gita puts it, "'I' gets swallowed up, without a trace, in the Self."

The discovery, then, is: "'You' are the Self. There is nothing *apart* from you," because you *are* the Self: there is but One thing, one inseparable reality.

"The rock-firm conviction of *'I am the Self'* is the sure mark of firm abidance in the Self." If this nondual principle is not unfailingly clear to you, you will not be in a position to understand the precepts which naturally follow from it.

In other words, if you don't comprehend that $0+0=0$, you won't appreciate that $10\text{x}0=0$. So, here's where the implications of "*all* is the Self" begin.

If you are the all-inclusive Self, you are not *instead*—or even *also*—'I'.

Where there is no I, there are no "other" things which (from a dualistic standpoint) we identify as pertaining to that I. Thus: "the experience of 'I am the Self' is the dissolution of the 'mind.'"

Just as the 'I' is a separative conception which is inapplicable in Self-awareness, all other *separative* conceptions are erroneous too. Said another way, if there is an I which is in actuality the Self, then the 'mind' of that I is *also* none other than the Self. The Gita says, thus: "All mental conceptions are nothing but the Self." So anything which one might conceive, identify in particular, or name (including *thinking* about such) presumes a "mind"—and the "mind" itself is another of these (separative) *conceptions*. From the standpoint of the (nondual) One, anything which can be conceived (or not conceived) is "nothing but the Self," since the Self is *all* that exists.

Such a precept cannot be intuited within any kind of a dualistic framework. It is stated: "there are no *mind* and *thought* forms, apart from the Self."

This means any and *all kinds* of thought forms, not just so-called "enlightened" thoughts, or "good" or positive thoughts. "All illusion exists in the Self only," is an example of the Gita's language. Where there is a "mind" in the illimitable Self, all the mind's "thoughts" must be the Self too.

The comprehension of this precept is indispensible for understanding the body of enlightenment teachings. All else will seem paradoxical otherwise.

Notice how the Gita dwells on this matter, among six verses:

> There is certainly no such thing as "mind," with its "objects".... The "thought" that the mind exists is the parent of all trouble and illusions. Abide in the conviction that there is no mind, with all its vagaries.... Denial of the existence of the mind is the conquest of the "mind".... There never was a mind. Who hears this great secret, and understands completely, abides as the Self.... In the conviction that "I am the Self," no thought, ego, mind or confusion can exist.... There is no such thing as the troublesome mind, no "world" of

names and forms, not the least bit of "ego." All these are nothing but the Self.

From the overall standpoint of nonduality, the dualistic perspective (which most everyone has been conditioned to, since infancy) is illusive. So, if all illusion exists as the Self, the dualist perspective too is not other than the One reality. To the extent that all we define *in*—or *as*—the "world" is a consequence of dualistic *differentiation*, the world too is the Self. Therefore, how "real" is the world as a "separate" form? After all, where the mind does not exist as a separate reality, how real are any of the "things" it is thought to conceive or perceive?

"There is no world, other than in the mind: upon [enlightenment] this 'mind' turns out to be nothing," is the point. Getting this point in full "destroys the ego-mind utterly, with all it afflictions....There is not an atom apart from the Self, which is the integral, undifferentiated whole Being."

Notice how emphatic the Gita is, concerning the foregoing precepts, in about a dozen of its verses:

> In the unitary Self, body, senses, mind, intellect (thought) are not apart from that sole Self....There is no such thing as a "person" lost in Samsara; everything that is seen to exist must be realized to be Self....All thought, all objects, all things heard, all questions and answers should be regarded as Self only....Ignorance and illusion, all beings and nonbeing, all bodies and the lives that arise in them are Self only....There is no such thing as objectives; efforts leading to them; acts of "practice"; the learner (disciple) or learned (guru);

or goals ("unification") achieved: What exists is only Self....

Be firm in the conviction that there are no charitable ("good") acts, no loss or gain, karma, bhakti ("worship"), knower ("you") or known ("god"). All these thought forms are bound to be dissolved in Self, the sole existence (or reality)....There is no creator, no maya (obscurance), no duality, no objects ("things") at all....The universe, name and form, creatures and creator, mind, desire, action are merely thought-formations....The sole Existence, without a "second," is the basic reality. The illusion of the "universe" is based on the mind, which again is an illusion.... The universe was neither born, nor maintained, nor dissolved; this is the plain truth...

Anything seen as other than Self is bound to cause trouble....The basic screen, devoid of all name and form, is the sole eternal Existence....Regard everything as Self only, until all thought of things "other" than the Self is lost.

Where there is only the Self, and hence you are the Self, there is not anything to be gained or gotten. That's why it's said the seeker is that which is being sought. Consequently, all efforts to "reach" the Absolute are pointless: you are already that which you would "unite" with.

All pilgrimages to "sacred" places and worship of gods must be firmly given up, in favor of the teachings (precepts)....All yogic practices, all philosophic pursuits, all devotional exercises, and all faiths and beliefs should be abandoned....One should give up all hatha yogic practices like breath control, all religious dogmas and their diverse sadhanas (paths) and be ever satisfied in simple abidance as the Self only.

All of these, too, are only That, already.

The residue of the empowerment of these teachings is what is sometimes called an empty—that is, placid or untroubled—awareness, "reduced to perfect stillness, after being freed from [divisive or separative] thought currents." It is the 'bliss" of what we'd call equanimity, also known as Samadhi.

> Abidance in the Self is the true nondual Samadhi....To abide still and blissful in that conviction is the acme of all sadhanas (paths), Samadhi as well....That state of still awareness is the state beyond compare, absolved from all "duties" (pursuits)....Free from traces of fear, "births" and "deaths," this is the fundamental truth.... The truth beyond all doubt, the truth declared by the Upanishads....

> Unbroken abidance in alert awareness, unruffled by thoughts, is Self–realization....consciousness completely dissolved in Self.

Those who've followed this far have likely considered that even the thought-forms of the "state" of "enlightenment," too, can be dispensed with. The names and forms we've used, like a stick to stir the fire of "emptiness"—such as "realization," "nondual," even "Self"—can now also be thrown into the fire.

One's abidance in awareness of the condition of *no thing* is essentially what has been given another [name and form] title: sahaja. "Consciousness freed from 'thoughts' will give up the *above* thought also....Even this *one* thought [I am That] must be given up, in order to abide firmly" in what is termed sahaja. "The sacrifice of the [name-and-form-giving] mind is, in fact, the totality of all sacred sacrifices."

> Remaining alertly aware with a still mind devoid of differentiation, even while engaged in "activities" of "worldly life," is called sahaja —natural (unimposed) abidance....Abidance in sahaja, peace is [present]....
> Having realized that the world picture on the screen (of awareness) is essentially nonexistent, even while functioning as an "individual" in the world of name and form, is called sahaja....Who [so] abides is rare to find....To find and gain access to the presence of such (as a Teacher) is the [most fortunate] that one could ever obtain....if one is keen on being released into freedom (sahaja).

Otherwise, one can "always dwell on the written words," such as the Ribhu Gita. "Why waste words: this is the truth in a nutshell; reading this leads to *peace*."

Reality is Present

You are the nation's president, and so the press photographers are waiting when you walk out of the hospital clinic after your annual physical exam. Back in your office that afternoon, you look at the photo on the front page of the newspaper. Your face appears blanched, taut, grim. You were told today that you have cancer.

Yesterday you were "well," today you are "sick." You look in your files for a campaign photo, of some months before: you are smiling, buoyant, glowing, in that photo.

You don't proceed to compare the two pictures. The campaign photo does not reflect a current reality; it is not a true picture of anything which is vital. There is not a separate reality—such as your "wellness"—which exists today. The past has no viable presence; and so it cannot be said that the existing situation is a "worsening" of a situation which does not even exist. You toss the campaign photo in the waste paper basket.

A few weeks later, you return to the hospital clinic. The cancer is surgically removed. The next day's newspaper photos show you waving cheerily as you return to your office.

Were you to now dig out your "sick" photo and compare it to today's "well" photo, and note your "improvement," you would be returning to the better/worse rollercoaster of contrasting the nonexistent to the existent.

The reality which exists is not a "better" or a "worse" reality: there is only one reality. To compare any other condition to the present condition is not a recognition of truth.

No Real Questions

Dear Robert:

What has happened since our talk is very present and there are no real questions.

Questions only arise when the dualistic perception reappears, but the questions do not last in the Absolute perspective.

So the truth appeared as a truth, and the "me and mine" dissolved in a laugh of full relief!

Life is the same, but the attitude to life has changed and become less personal, or not personal at all. Sitting in nature is a strong new drive, Paris's gardens for now.

At the sea in Greece in front of the ocean it was all so clear, the ocean and the waves...there are no independent waves, only the ocean; no life, no death, just the appearance or disappearance of a motion in the ocean itself.

That understanding I go back to often...

Before the realization, I always thought that I will have things to say to other people but now there is not anymore a me who wants to say or prove anything— there is just not a me separate from them, and there are no words to express this state.

In a way, the "teaching" is simply: That talking to Itself!

Thanks for your report. What you are noticing is that there is ultimately only one answer to every question which arises: It's just another appearance of the Absolute.

And with clarity now, you are finding a dimension to meditation which you would not have known before the emptiness. In that emptiness, as you say, no life, no death.

Get Real

Asked what is the major lesson of the spiritual teachings, I'd have to say that it is *impermanence.*

As Ramana Maharshi points out, all forms (whether material or immaterial) arise then dissipate; they are impermanent. The actuality in which they originate and subside is infinite and eternal, and is itself without form. Thus, this ground of being is the only element which is not impermanent. Ultimately, as Ramana says, this Being-ness is the only lasting reality.

In Buddhism, it is emphasized that "all *things* change." That formless reality, which is not one of the nameable things, and which is not limited by time or space, is the Unchanging.

The spiritual teachings urge us to focus attention on what is permanent and ever present (which Ramana would call *real*), rather than on the ephemeral, the fleeting forms (which Ramana calls *unreal*).

The ultimate reality is said to be the source of all that is; and, as such, is what all the relative things hold in common. What the enlightened masters perceive is *sameness*, the essence which links "the ten thousand things" in unity, Oneness. The sage perceives this indivisible essence as one's true nature. It was "your face before you were born"; your form appeared in this empty presence, and will disappear into it—the ground of being remaining entirely unaffected. From the standpoint of the Ultimate, each "individual life" is meaningless.

The recognition of impermanence places petty, self-generated concerns in their proper perspective. It leaves attention undistracted, to contemplate each unsecured moment in awareness that it may be the viewer's last.

Pick up a newspaper any day, and you'll read about someone who walked out their front door that morning and never returned. Nonexistence for an organism may be only one breath away. You might rinse your wine glass this evening and never fill it again.

Paul Krassner once told me, "The central fact of my life is my death." To live one's life not taking any of its conditions complacently for granted is to appreciate the presence which is manifest. It is, as Krishnamurti titled one of his books, *A Wholly Different Way of Living*. It is to have incorporated the teachings regarding impermanence.

The Infinite Supply Co.

A bean, planted in the ground, sits still, and what it needs is given to it. Without "planning" to, it gives itself over to a succession of roots, leaves, blossoms and fruitful pods. Itself passively transformed by energy, it is thereby an instrument of energy; this energy is intelligence: and this intelligence is the cause of life and the cause of death. Intelligence trans-forms.

Chuang tzu: "The destruction of life does not mean death; nor the prolongation of life an addition to the 'duration' of one's *existence*."

Every particle, however minuscule (and every wave, however insignificant) knows precisely what to do, at every instant and point in time or space. There is a word for this: omniscience. If all particles are infinitely intelligent, and every thing is composed of particles, then all things are intelligent (or, intelligence is all things). And it would not be proper to say that this is intelligence operating "within" Intelligence: there is but one intelligence.

Intelligence is not separate from a single molecule; and this intelligence is undivided from each and every other molecule. No molecule is more the cause or the effect of this intelligence.

We seem conditioned to conceive of order only from without, not order from within—spontaneous, "unordered" order, the order of bubbles in sea foam. We cannot compose an equation which embodies chaos and intelligence and order. We cannot envision something that autonomously originates without preference and automatically perpetuates without choice. The profound (and singular) miracle is the miracle of auto genesis.

Astrophysicist Paul Davies affirms of the Big Bang, "the initial singularity is truly an effect without a prior cause; for there is no pre-existing space or time—or anything physical at all—to contain this 'cause'."

Stuart Atkinson, an astronomer, says succinctly of the Big Bang, "if *everything* that exists came from it, then nothing could have existed before it."

This would seem to be obvious. Not until -10^{43} seconds after moment zero was the substance (which expanded to produce the cosmos) even as large as an atom's nucleus. (Or, as Atkinson describes it):

> "In the first fraction of a fraction of a billionth of a second after the Big Bang, our universe was compressed into a tiny sphere smaller than the point of a needle."

Clearly, given this density of mass, no "space" was yet available. And, since time is essentially a descriptive concept for measuring distance, there would have been no "things" in relationship which could be calibrated by time. Even though scientists speak, for convenience, of the relative time of the explosive event, neither time nor space (nor gravity) could have had any possible reality at all until Atkinson's so-called "tiny sphere" had eventually ripped itself asunder.

On an astronomical level, it seems to be similar to a proton emitting a "virtual" pion, "spontaneously out of the void," as Fritjof Capra says, "formed out of nothing."

The Absolute as Reality

There are two manifestations of immediate interest to us here: Wyatt and Robert (hereinafter referred to as "you," and "I" or "me"). Both are manifestations of the same Reality. We are manifestations of this Reality not only physically (one body there, one body here), but in terms of everything that physicality experiences as well. In other words, what we consider to be "our" ("yours" or "my") mind is as much the manifestation, a "form" of the Formless, as is the body with which it is presumed to be associated. Therefore, the thoughts, emotions, reactions, reflections, etc., of this organism ("me") and that organism ("you") are nothing more than manifestations of the same, one Reality.

This Reality expresses itself, is manifest (takes form), uniquely in each form it takes: snowflake, planet, body, etc. And, yet, not any single one of these forms ever remains unchanging. (Miracle?!)

The perspective of *this* organism, while similar to your own in some ways, is in some ways different from yours. Reality's reflection on Reality (or, on "itself") is somewhat different, as a result of the experience of *this* organism, than is Reality's reflection on Reality in "your" instance.

Reality is simply doing what it does. Manifesting. And changing manifestation. All that *is*, is merely *that*: Reality manifest as change.

How this changing Reality has manifested—our "experience"—affects our perspective. And our perspective affects our experience. Both are merely manifestations of the same, single Reality.

From the standpoint of Reality, obviously, both are okay. *And* the potential for change *either* way exists—such as the potential for *this* organism to affect *that* organism.

Open completely to the discovery of what is *animating* the bodily forms, on both sides of your door. There can be only one *Real*-ity.

I am not talking about striving for the union of anything; not anything has ever been *dis*united, from the beginning. When the notion of disunity has fallen aside, the quandaries expressed in your letters find their resolution. All of the things that are happening, are happening to "you." What is the Reality that animates this form, referred to as you? What is it that activates all that is in relationship, in one way or another, *to* you? The same Reality?

This in no way denies that what is happening *is* happening. Reality is manifesting, and Reality is changing. The question is: are you apart from the Reality that manifests and changes; or are you simply another aspect (manifestation) of that very Reality? Could that "perspective of how the thing is being viewed," as you say in your letter, have any affect on the *conflict* you experience?

The Reality that has no form of its own (by whatever name you wish to call it) is behind *all* that *is*—without a single exception.

That is sitting here writing a letter to *itself*. To Reality, there are no "miles" between "us"; no "writer," no "reader"; no thoughts that are "yours" or "mine."

Hardware as Image

One of the things which makes spiritual traditions mystical is their concurrence on the paradoxical aspect of revelation.

We believe the world and its objects to be real. How is it said that they are *unreal*?

Put another way, most people have no doubt that the material manifestations are real, but have great doubt as to whether the embodied presence of the Absolute is real.

That which is real, in the context of the sages, is *always* real—unchanged throughout eternity. All that is created and destroyed—even primordial solar systems—are *not* real.

All that is impermanent comes and goes, in the context of a backdrop that is *without* beginning or ending. An analogy that has been given is that of the progression of movie footage on a *screen*, which supports the activity without movement on its own part.

In the case of universal manifestation, the background is without form, whereas all things which appear as contrast on the background *have* form, and each 'thing' is *limited* to its form.

Since the unlimited formless is what is fundamentally real, it has to be the *ground* which gives rise—en potentia—to all that is materially manifest.

In other words, the forms are dependent upon the formless for their arising; the impermanent exists on a lattice of the permanent.

But, just as the 'unreal' cannot exist without the real, the real has no *appearance* of existence without the unreal. The formless has no *existence* objectively, without taking form.

The impermanent things are the forms through which the formless experiences its reality. They are the *immanent* presence of the *transcendent* presence ("God's *image*").

"You," as an individual, are one of the unreal forms superimposed on the backdrop of the real. As a *manifestation* of the formless, you are not *separate* from the formless; the real and the unreal, being inseparable, are in actuality simply one whole, complete actuality; so you are not entirely *un*real.

The unreal cannot *appear* to our consciousness without the *existence* of the real. The formless Real is not merely a presence *around* the unreal; it is a real presence in and *through* all that is.

All that we see can be viewed as Real or unreal, depending on the perspective: "half full, or half empty." But the point is: *both; not two.*

That tree is real. And it is unreal. It surpasses either category. Your body-mind is unreal; your formless presence is unchangingly real.

Ramana:

"Shankara says

Brahman is real;

the Universe is unreal;

Brahman is the Universe...."

Ramana explains:

"The Universe is conceived to be apart from Brahman (by the unenlightened), and that perception is wrong....

"A mirage does not *disappear*, even after one's knowing it to be a mirage: the *envisioned* is still there—but the person does not run to it for water....The world is an illusion. Even after knowing that, it continues to appear. It must be known to be *Brahman*, and not apart.

"If the world appears, *to whom* does it appear... the Self. Otherwise, would the world appear in the *absence* of the Self? Therefore, the Self, is the reality. The phenomena are real (only) *as the Self*; and are illusions (when) *apart from* the Self....That is what is meant by 'reality and unreality' being one and the same....

"A phenomenon cannot be a reality simply because it serves a (practical) purpose. Take a dream, for example; they serve a purpose.

"Dream *water* quenches dream *thirst*. The dream creation, however, is contradicted in the waking state.

"The waking creation ("real world") is contradicted in the other two states (while in a dream, or in deep sleep)....If real, a thing must *ever* be real; and not real for a short time and unreal at other times....

"Similarly, the universe cannot be real of itself: that is to say, apart from the *underlying* Reality."

Supreme Be-ing

Even persons who are acquainted with the historic literature on nonduality (especially English translations) are often familiar with only a few of the terms which are traditionally given in Sanskrit. *Advaita*, which means "not two," would probably be at least one of those known.

An important word, *Samadhi*, is one of the least understood. It refers generally to what we might think of as a state of consciousness, and it is characterized in basically three "stages." The first two relate to an effortful or deliberate *intent*, but whose *achievement* remains impermanent.

Savikalpa, the initial phase (also sometimes called *Kevala*, which Ramana Maharshi defines as "practitioner") is when the aspirant for Self-realization has grasped the insight that "Brahman and I are the same actuality." Howerver, in this perspective, there still remains an idea that there *is* an "I" and a "Brahman" which can conceivably coalesce to become a "One"; in other words, there is still a subtle sense of duality in the aspirant's mind.

Nirvikalpa is the state whereby the aspirant's view would have enlarged to, "all is Brahman." But this recognition is temporary, it "comes and goes." For example, this might dominate one's awareness when sitting in meditation, but at varying times later—"back in real life"—the unitive awareness is occluded.

Beyond Nirvakalpa is *Sahaja*, which means "natural"— in the sense of ordinary (Buddhists would say, "nothing special" about it). Such distinctions even as "all" and "Brahman" are transcended: "Not two, not one," as the Vedas say. Since "there is nothing from the start," there need be no effort to achieve or retain any *particular* state of awareness. Sometimes also termed *Sahaja nirvikalpa samadhi* (or simply *Sahaja Samadhi*), it is the embodiment of Self-realization (or enlightenment) which we would phrase as Absolute awareness.

If you're looking for an equivalent for the word *Samadhi*, it is not "trance," it is not "bliss," it is "embodiment" of Self-realization. The word *enlightenment* could be a replacement, too, where Ramana states, "Samadhi alone can reveal the truth."

If you were looking for a subsidiary word, you could apply *clarity*. "The tranquil clarity, which is devoid of mental turmoil, alone is the samadhi which is the firm base for liberation."

And anything conceived as samadhi which is lesser than, or short of, sahaja is not the full extent of samadhi. "Those that are in the kevala nirvikalpa state are not realized, they are still seekers."

The seeker still retains a dualistic bias, however subtle. He will suppose that there is a someone (even himself) who is somehow apart from ultimate Reality: and by doing (or not doing) something, the gap can be closed and "union" result. But: "Remaining in the primal, pure natural state *without effort* is sahaja nirvikalpa samadhi."

An attempt to "close the gap" through "practice" is not what Ramana means by the "natural state." For instance,

"Meditation is initiated and sustained by a conscious effort of the mind. When such effort entirely subsides, it is called samadhi.... Meditation is a forced mental process, whereas samadhi lies beyond effort.... The *cosmic* mind, being not limited by the ego, has nothing separate from itself."

There is no "individual" who is somehow apart from the Absolute, or Self.

It is not about falling into a temporary trance, or experiencing an orgasmic or "oceanic" bliss: rather, it is the dissolution of the subjective "self," and its person-alized identity, into the awareness of the inescapable presence of infinite Be-ing. "When we are always in that state, not going *into* samadhi and coming *out* again, that is the sahaja state. In sahaja, one sees only the Self..."

It is when one is "*merging* in the one Reality underlying all the phenomena, the Being which is the one reality giving rise to all thoughts, this state is said to be sahaja...You realize that you are moved by the deeper Self within, and are *unaffected by what you do or say or think*...and that *everything is being done by something* with which you are in conscious union...One who...will not lose his samadhi state...whatever external work he does, and whatever thought may come to him—that is called sahaja...

Ramana says the naïve idea that samadhi is a dropping into and out of unconsciousness would matter not, even if it were true: *whatever* state or condition of observable existence, it is a manifest expression of the Self, or Being.

"What does it matter whether body consciousness is lost or retained? *When lost, it is samadhi; when retained, it is samadhi*: that is all. ...If those who have all the Upanishads and vedantic tradition at their disposal have fantastic notions about nirvikalpa, who can blame a westerner for similar notions? ...Samadhi is one's *natural* state. It is the undercurrent in all the three states of waking, dreaming, and sleeping."

Ramana emphasizes that sahaja is the awareness that the seer (I) and the seen (other) are always and only *one*, or Self: the nondual (rather than the dualistic) perspective. Those in that state "cannot find anything which is different from themselves. But to those who do not reach that state, everything appears to be different from themselves.... In the perfect state, there is neither subject nor object: there is nothing [apart] to see...

> "A strong conviction that 'I am the Self' is necessary, *transcending* 'mind' and *all* phenomena.... The artificial 'I' is a projection, and through it one must look to the true Principle.... One has to know what samadhi is. And how can you know it without knowing your Self? If the Self is known, *samadhi* will be known automatically.... To be one's own Self is *samadhi*. The Absolute consciousness is our real nature.... What is samadhi? : one's own *true nature*.... In that state, there is Being, alone. There is no you, nor I, nor it; no present, nor past, nor future. It is beyond time and space, beyond expression [thought]. It is *ever here*....
>
> "Samadhi is holding onto the Reality while witnessing the world, without reacting to it from within—the stillness of a waveless ocean.... Consciousness which is Absolute and unaffected: that is samadhi.... Sages say that the state of equilibrium which is devoid of the ego is samadhi."

Someone posed to Ramana: "It is said in the Mandukya Upanishad that samadhi must necessarily be experienced before attaining liberation."

Ramana replied, "It is stated not only in the Mandukya Upanishad but in all the ancient books. But it is *true* samadhi only if you know your Self."

The Ribhu Gita, which Ramana sometimes quoted, says: "Remaining alertly aware...devoid of differentiation [duality]—even while being engaged in the activities of worldly life—is called the state of sahaja samadhi: the natural state of abidance in the Self."

The (female) jnani Mata Amritanandamayi:

> "By meditating on a form, savikalpa samadhi (perception of the Real while retaining the sense of *duality*) can be attained. When one sees the *form* of the beloved Deity, the attitude of 'I' is there, thus there is duality."

> "In the state of *nirvikalpa* samadhi there is no entity to say '*I* am *Brahman*'."

> "In 'formless meditation' [sahaja]; since there is no trace of 'I-ness', the attitude of duality is completely destroyed."

> "What will samadhi be like? *No happiness or sorrow.* There is no 'I' and 'you'. This state can be compared *to deep sleep*, but there is a difference. In samadhi, there is full awareness. Only when we wake up, I, you, and the world emerge. We give reality to them due to our ignorance."

Muruganar, a poet, and awakened disciple of Ramana:

> "To remain in the state in which consciousness of the supreme Reality is not lost, even during activities, is sahaja.... Sahaja (is the) state that exists...in such

a way that it is not possible to *separate* from it.... Without desirelessness [un-intention], the abiding experience of sahaja samadhi will not ripen.... Until that state of sahaja...there is no liberation for the individual, irrespective of what *other* state one may experience."

A later follower of Ramana, David Godman:

"Sahaja *means* 'natural'...the *direct* experience of the Self, in which no differences or *distinctions* arise. Sahaja nirvikalpa samadhi is the *definitive* state of realization, in which one can live a normal—*natural*—life, fully aware of the Self at all times....

"Experience of Realization is known as samadhi. It is often supposed that samadhi implies trance, but that is not necessarily so. It is also possible to be in a state of samadhi while retaining full possession of human faculties. In fact, a Self-realized sage (such as the Maharshi) is permanently in such a state...

"When one is established in one's true state, one knows the Truth by direct experience. Such a one is 'sahaja nishta', one who is established in the natural state of the Self."

Ramana, in summary:

"The sahaja state: that is realization, for certain.... The *ever-present* state is the *natural* state, sahaja.... The reason for...emphasizing sahaja samadhi (is that) one should be in *spontaneous* samadhi—that is, in one's pristine state—in the midst of every environment.... The Absolute consciousness is our real nature.... Samadhi (is) one's own true nature."

Desire's Journey

Everybody was saying goodbye to Mick. He had come to the RV park three years before, fresh out of jail. A burly, barrel-chested man, he had, for twenty-five years, made a precarious living with his hands and his fists. His previous "job," before his incarceration, had been as a bouncer in a blue-collar bar; as long as he remained sober enough to control the crowd of "serious drinkers," he was given pocket money, his meals, a place to park his live-in camper, and all he could drink.

He had been the target of gunshot, a few times, in his "work," and in his last skirmish he had exacted a painful toll from his antagonist, to the extent that he was imprisoned. Now, a free agent once again, but humble, sober and hungry for the first time in his adult life, he was given a job as the RV campground's handyman. Not long after, he married one of the single women there.

His brother, who lived in Arkansas, had been a carpenter; he suddenly came into a handsome sum of money, due to an accident. For his vacation, Mick and his wife took their camper, and their dog, and visited the brother. Shortly after their return to California, the brother phoned: "You remember that piece of property you were admiring, the one with the big motor home on it? I bought it for you!"

"Jesus Christ! Why the hell did you do that?!"

"You're my brother, and I love you, and I want you to be near." He paused. "Three years ago, I never thought I'd be saying that."

"Me neither. But you're way out in the boonies; I'd need a four-wheel-drive to live there, and I'd be snowed in for a whole month during winter. How the hell would I make a living?"

"You remember meeting Graham Parker? He said he likes you, and you can work for him. He cuts firewood, all year around. And there's a four-by-four that goes with the job; all you have to do is buy your own gas when you go into Redway to shop."

"I've got to finish out my month here, to get my pay. Tell Parker I'll be wearing my new work boots on the first day of next month!"

Mick's wife was on the way out to walk the dog, when the phone had rung. She had sat down next to him on the sofa, and had heard the conversation. When Mick hung up the phone, she said: "I ain't going."

Mick lit a cigarette. "A man's gotta do what a man's gotta do!"

"And a woman's gotta do what a woman's gotta do," she said, following the dog out the door. "I ain't going."

Mick stubbed out his cigarette, and said aloud to himself, "*She* ain't going! *She* ain't *going*!"

Now Mick was packing his tools in his camper, and various people at the campground were coming by to shake his hand and wish him well.

He set out that night, so as to cross the desert quickly. At 2 a.m., he wanted a cup of coffee; the only place he came to was a roadhouse.

"We ain't got no coffee made," the barkeep said, "but I can brew a pot. Take probably ten minutes."

"I'm in a hurry."

"Then how about a glass of beer?"

"Shit! Okay."

Leaving the roadhouse an hour later, Mick was arrested for driving on the wrong side of the road, speeding, and drunk driving. He was also in violation of parole.

He returned to the campground humble, sober and hungry. His brother had wired the bail money, and Mick was again working at his old job—but now as "assistant" care-taker—until his court date and return to jail.

And everyone was stopping to say goodbye to Mick.

Whatever There Is

All of anything which can be conceived of as "time" is, in an undivided cosmos, wholly present now. Any "process" in time, such as "change," is—rather than continuous—simultaneous, spontaneous. In other words, "cause" is not at some specific point, in this immeasurable universe, and "effect" at some other designated point.

As with man's other concepts, the trouble begins when an attempt is made to identify and isolate cause and effect from a field in which there is no division, which is to say no separable thing, event or phenomenon. It is only our conception of time which permits such a conception as cause or effect.

There is no cause, nor is there an effect, except to the mind which confines itself within limits. Where there is no cause and no effect, "change," too, can be but another of man's conceptual constructs. In a cosmos in which all things are essentially the same ("one") thing, change can be only a movement of energy amongst itself...in a field of energy. And it is not even a movement, if there is admittedly not the element of time with which to measure it. Put another way, all change can be nothing more than meaningless from the "cosmic" viewpoint.

Given man's supposition that there is an activity which can be specified as change, there is no place where he cannot locate it. And given that all "things" *are* "change," his attempts to anticipate and control it are vain. Control cannot even *appear* to be a reality, outside of his fabricated matrix of time and the presumed causes and effects that it alleges to chronicle.

The supposition of cause and effect is interdependent with our presumption of "subject" versus "object"—the individuated self as subject, in a "relationship" to such things or objects as "others," "time," "reality," "death." To the mind which posits such divisive, polarized concepts as "life" versus "death," or "better" and "worse," the singular Presence is stretched to the breaking point on the continuum of time/change. Man then attempts a failed harmony between such dualities as pleasure and pain. Thus man chronically views things and events in terms of the way they ought to be, or ought not to be, rather than perceiving the most simple and obvious of actualities: whatever there is, it is the way it is.

Untethered Mind

Our thinking, typically, is purposely "logical," or linear, and as such it is limited: it permits us concrete exposure to only three dimensions and five senses. Discovering that logic is limited, we logically limit our reliance on it. How is one to function in an irrational world, as long as one depends on rationality?

Is thought a product of the mind, any more than the mind is a product of thought? Does the brain think—or is it thought which alleges that the brain thinks? Thought being limited, does it fail to recognize how utterly limited it is? In the same way that the accuracy of words is established only by other words, the legitimacy of thought is confirmed only by thought. "Reason" is whatever reasoning says that it is.

Originally, the words *think* and *thing* were related. It is "things" which "think," and it is things that are thought about. There is no tomorrow, without thought; but the thought of tomorrow is not tomorrow. In the same way that we attempt to name every object ("thing"), we attempt to name every event ("think"); whatever we name, changes— and so we name the changes. This is "reasonable," or "logical," we suppose. We have come to believe that the event or change was isolated, in form, *before* we named it ("tomorrow").

What do you need to know, in this very moment? Thought, knowledge, information could lead to truth only if truth was a conclusion. Though truth might be said to be a fact, all the facts in existence, added together, do not total the Truth. Open the mind, and empty it. Come not to a comma or colon, but to an ellipse...

A light appears in the dark, of an instant, and you glimpse what you have not seen before; it may, or may not, appear again, but you are now aware of its existence—not as a vision in the speculative mind, but as a sight of truth. Before Einstein had explanations, he had insight. This is not the same as to "reflect" on truth; reflection is an indirect experience, a seeing delayed by time and space, the same time and space occupied with thought.

To end self-centered thought is a change of mind. And we arrive at this ending through awareness, not through thought. It is not that thinking per se is eliminated, it is that awareness transforms thought—freeing it from its pattern of speculation and calculation—so that it is ended as we normally know it. We could say that thought is *form*, and awareness is *void*; and the balanced relationship of the two is reestablished. Understanding the true nature of the linear mind and of the non-linear mind, one understands how to use which, and when. And one stops depending upon thought to explore and express that which is beyond thought, that which is capable of finding expression without thought.

As long as awareness is what you think it is, it is thought and not awareness. Awareness is not a matter of speculative choice. It is more a process than a product. It is a letting go. It is awareness of our "normal" unawareness, our chronic inattention to the present. It is awareness without really trying. Awareness is perception is wholeness. Into this wholeness, when present, all added information fits effortlessly.

Being present in the moment, the moment changes—and we change with it, without friction, without resistance. The moment is not ideal: can we be at peace with that? Not "can we accept that?"; can we be at peace with even what we cannot accept? We live in a culture which is resistant to—unaccepting of—change...and yet we long personally for inner change (peace) and collectively for social change (brotherhood).

Concomitant with awakening is attention—awareness—in the moment; calculative thought is inattention in the moment, un-awareness. To be attentive only to the moment represents a radical shift, from our normal way of life.

Follow the moment to the very end, and you will come to that place where you truly reside now, as a native. This is not a place which thought will lead you to, thought will rather lead you away from it. Can peace possibly be something which is isolated from the other activities or processes in your life? As Alan Watts has said of perception, it is "being aware of life without thinking about it...then carrying this on even while one is thinking."

Fully attentive to the present moment, there is none other to compare it with. Awareness cannot exist except in the present. It is when thought has been stripped away that intelligence operates. It is through letting go that we learn the truth of who we really are—and *then* thought can find its necessary expression. To know thyself, be attentive from moment to moment; why are you doing what you're doing? "The Self is realized," said Ramana Maharshi, "not by one's doing something, but by one's refraining from doing anything—*by remaining still and being simply what one really is.*" This is not a realm of opportunity for calculative and speculative thought.

While there may not likely be a dramatic change in mankind's consciousness anytime soon, there can be a critical change in your consciousness—immediately. It is possible for each of us to be a source of the profound energy that transform the lives of others. But that source is not issued from second-hand revelation, but from first-hand perception and awareness.

Nothing Doing

You wrote:

> "*All* attempts at control of a situation (any situation) is a failure to trust That which Does. Control and idealism are closely related: the latter gives birth to the former."

You got *that* right.

Concerning the other matter you mentioned: Yes, some teachers speak as if we had a choice (such as to seek enlightenment), while others say we've never had any choice about anything (and they don't mean this in the sense of "predestination").

Actually, all true enlightenment teachers want you to be aware that there is a possibility for each of us to transcend such ideational concerns as "choice/no choice." What does it matter? If you posit that there is a choice, you will then do what you do. If you assert that there is no choice, you will proceed to do what you do.

We could say that if there is a choice, it is "you" who makes the choice. If there is no you, we might tend to assume that something "other" is directing the choice. In absence of the idea of a "you" *or* an "other," there is simply what is taking place.

Animals seem to make choices; yet they appear to have no capacity for an internal debate: "Am *I* choosing to make this decision, or is something *else* doing it for me?"

Awareness of one's actions need not lead to the question "why?" The "why?" is based on the self-conscious quandary "am I doing the *right* thing, or the *wrong* thing?"

As with an animal, you will do what you will do. Some observers will judge your action as "fitting," in the circumstances, others as "unfitting." Some will opine that you had a choice, others that you had no choice. Some will be of no opinion, and will observe that it's simply "what's happening."

We *grant* that for animals. We hardly ever are so charitable to ourselves.

Gita Guide

The Avadhuta Gita (a.k.a. Song of the Free) was composed at an unknown time, ascribed to Dattatreya, of whom nothing is known. An English translation, from Sanskrit, by Swami Ashokananda (d. 1969) dates back to 1946. One virtue is that it is devoid of many of the Hindu terms which are so often difficult to translate from the original.

The word *avadhuta* refers to someone who has realized their identity with the Absolute; that is, whose perspective is nondual, known as Self-realized; enlightened. This particular gita was often quoted by Swami Vivekananda.

Like other gitas, it might have been written by a teacher of nonduality, for study by a follower. However, it reads like a collection of contemplative observations or notes, inscribed over a period of time. A typical line or two might touch on, say, three important precepts (which might take the rishi several hours to verbally explain). Even at best, statements might seem to be contradictory; certainly paradoxical: in other words, best understood by someone who no longer needs to read it.

Contextually, these teachings are as marrow in the bones of *advaita* (which means "not two"), called *ajata* (which could be said to be "not even one"). The point here is that ultimate reality is emptiness, nothingness: nothing from the start (a-jata translates as "no creation").

The teachings are along the line of what's known as "neti, neti": the *ultimate* reality is "not this, nor *this*." It is possible to spontaneously end spiritual seeking simply by contemplating and adhering to—giving full attention to—ajata's absolute perspective, with unequivocal consistency.

The excerpts which follow, taken from Ashokananda's rendering, are commented on now to give meaning to some of the subtler precepts. (For the sake of discursive clarity, the gita quotes used here do not appear in their order, and are connected together for topical continuity.)

One must *first* grasp the nature—emptiness—of ultimate reality: *no-thing*.

From the standpoint of duality, we could say there is *something* and there is *nothing*. From this point of view, before there is anything, there must be something which is not anything: nothing. We've long intuited that before we have one, two and three, etc, we have zero.

In this context, we cannot speak of *nothing* as having a beginning or an ending. This nothing is boundless, without borders. As such, it cannot be moved from where it is, to where it isn't. As nothing, it isn't any *where*. In fact, as nothing, it could as well be said that no where is it *not*.

Also, as nothing, it is not divisible; one can't say that it is *here*, but not *there*. While we can't say that it is *in* something, we cannot say that it is *not* in something; it does not present in "parts."

It defies, or transcends, such descriptions as *being* or *not being*, therefore as acting or not acting. Nothingness *precedes* all (dualistic) eventualities.

As such, it is said that the *somethingness* is superimposed on the nothingness.

The empty boundlessness is also referred to as the All (as in All-encompassing). It also is called Oneness, or even Truth.

But the word *all* is sometimes also used to speak of the "many," in distinction to the One. Somethingness *is*, of course, *in* the All.

So, this is how the ancient enlightenment teachers tried to characterize the nothingness which is at the base of ultimate reality. But the summation, in terms of *ultimate reality*, is that emptiness is the fundamental condition of reality; *ultimate reality* is empty of *every* thing. The gita says:

> Here *is only the absolute Truth, indivisible, and the All. The Self* [i.e, One] *transcends all, is indivisible and all–pervading. Space is pervaded by It, but It is not pervaded by anything. It is existing within and without. It is undivided and continuous. It has neither come, nor gone. It is without beginning, middle and end. Know all this 'universe'* [the 'many'] *to be of the nature of the Absolute. The whole universe shines undivided and unbroken.*

While nothingness is not something, in order to say anything about it, one has to talk about some *thing*. So, if we say that nothingness is formless—without boundaries, and thereby everywhere present whether inward or outward— that implies that it is present inside and outside all *forms*: "One is in all (the many); all is in One." Then, while there can be no distinctions within the unbroken Absolute, dualistic distinctions must be employed in order for us to say *anything* about the (nondual) nothingness.

The formless does not "come and go"; without beginning or end, it admits of no such limitation as finite time: the word *eternal* actually means 'beyond time,' or time-less. *Forms* come and go, are impermanent, are within the limiting confines of time. Thus, the precedent formlessness is said to be *real*, in the sense of everlasting; that which is not everlasting (all forms, e.g. the world) are thereby "unreal." But from the standpoint of (nondual) ajata, neither "real" nor "unreal" can be applied to nothingness.

Such a denial (of even the explanatory comparisons in advaita) is what makes comprehending a gita's statements so paradoxical, unavoidably: relative terms are utilized to discuss the non-relative; though the fundamental principle is that relative/nonrelative is a non-sequitur, in nothingness.

Consider the following from the standpoint of "not two": to speak of "relative" and "transcendental" (Absolute), or of "union" and "separation," is to posit (despite its useful purpose) that there are such (dual and separative) "states."

> *How shall I speak of the transcendental and relative states? How shall I speak of union and separation? Know that which has form to be false, that which is formless to be eternal. (The Self), devoid of life and lifelessness, shines forever.*

Even a reference to "I" suggests that there's some thing(s) which are "not-I."

> *This is my certain perception: I neither perform nor enjoy past action, future action, or present action. I was not born, nor have I death. I have no action, good or evil.*

So, the *substantive* statements of the Avadhuta Gita are from the (ajata) standpoint of "not even one".

> *It is ignorance to see difference in the Undifferentiated. If God pervades all, if God is immovable, undivided, then I see no division. The Self is that in which the*

distinction of teacher and disciple disappears, and in which the consideration of instruction also disappears. There is no distinction of the different and nondifferent. If there is only one indivisible, all-comprehensive Absolute, how can there be the comparable, and the comparison? There are never any 'you' and 'I'.

Some seek nonduality, others duality. They do not know the Truth, which is the same at all times and everywhere, which is devoid of both duality and nonduality. All is verily the absolute Self. Distinction and nondistinction do not exist. There is no distinction of within, without, or a junction of the two. There is nothing here which pervades or is pervaded. There is no state of liberation, no state of bondage, no state of perfection and no state of destitution. No such change as "greed and freedom from greed" exists. How can I say, "It exists; it does not exist"?

As seen, there are relative statements concerning nothingness; and absolute statements, among which the disclaimers are: It is not this, *and* it is not *this.* Since most of the venerated teachings include "not two" pointers along with "not even one," it is obvious that both emphases have their proper usage.

The main point which every teaching intends to convey, to a seeker of ultimate reality, is that he or she does not exist—in the most fundamental, or *real* sense—as some *thing*: There's *nothing* from the start.

This point is that every—impermanent—*thing* which arose from nothingness, subsides in nothingness.

When our avadhuta says, "I am free of illusion," it's because he (or she) recognizes that the all-unifying common source is nothingness. All forms arise in nothingness and subside in nothingness, and are as illusions, not "real," in between. In nothing, there are no illusions.

Coming to realize that the "self," all selves, and the worldly and cosmic background are unreal, in the most meaningful sense, is the essence of Self-realization.

> *I am free from illusion—my form has been extinguished. Know me, beyond all doubt, to be boundless. Know me, beyond all doubt, to be undivided. Know me to be that Self who is everything and everywhere at all times; who is eternal, the All, the nonexistent, and the Existent. Have no doubt.*
>
> *When the pot is broken, the space within is absorbed in the infinite space, and becomes undifferentiated. As the space within a pot dissolves in the universal space, when the pot is broken, so a yogi....dissolves into the supreme Self, which is his true being. Where there is such a natural Being, how can there be "I"; how can there be even "you"; how can there be the world? There is no you, no me, nor is there this universe. All is verily the Self alone. Thus you are One. You are the auspicious One existing everywhere at all times. Thou hast no name and form, even to the extent of allusion; nor any substance, differentiated or undifferentiated. You need not be ashamed to say, "I am the Self, the supreme Truth."*

Where, in the ultimate sense, there are no *individuals*, there are no individual *minds*: no "self," no "mind" of a self. If there *were* a mind, where *all* is the one Being, it would be *Being's* mind.

The avadhuta therefore views thought; words leading from those thoughts; and actions leading from words and thoughts, all as expressions of the one Being. He does not regard the self as the "thinker of thoughts" or the "doer of deeds." Where there is no independent self, there are not independent thoughts or independent deeds. "I am not the doer... How can I have a sense of 'my-ness'?"

> *If there is only one indivisible, all-comprehensive Absolute, how can there be consciousness differentiated by exterior and interior? I do not perceive any difference between the mind and the supreme Being.*
>
> *The Self is here in the universal Consciousness which is the All, and undivided. It is here in the universal Consciousness which is absolute and immovable. The Mind is indeed the indivisible, all-comprehensive Absolute.*

Where there is no individual self, there is no self to improve, perfect or change. Such a one does not progress from a "stained" or "defiled" state, to an "unstained" or "undefiled state." Therefore, for this one, there are no *practices, rituals, purifications, renunciations* etc. One does not retain a hope of attaining any experience which the self receives as a result of "devotion," "discipline," "controlling the mind and senses," and so forth.

One's uncontrived, natural condition is what the Self-realized know as Beingness. We need make no effort to simply abide as Being. And we need not even be told "how" to *do* that.

I am not the worshipper, or of the form of the worshipped. I have neither instruction, nor practice. Even my natural self appears to me as non-distinct from the supreme Self; it appears to be one, and like space. How can there be meditator and meditation?.... How can there be any accomplishment through meditation...There is no meditator or meditation. The wise, my child, give up all meditations...knowing this, one never says that the yogis have any particular 'path.' For them it is the giving up of all duality. He attains the supreme, eternal Self whether he has perfect self-control or not, whether he has withdrawn his senses or not, whether he has gone beyond activity or is active.

A major consequence of Self-realization is the dissolution of the fear of death: that of which there has been "nothing from the start" does not die; one merely subsides into one's original, "unborn" condition.

The supreme Reality is the state of the highest serenity. For you, there is no birth or death. Neither is there an individual soul nor the form of an individual soul. The Self is the negation of death and deathlessness. It is the negation of action and inaction. If there is only one indivisible, all-comprehensive Absolute, how can one speak of coming and going? In whatever place yogis "die," in whatever state, there they "dissolve" [becoming indistinguishable from the Self], *as the space of a jar dissolves into the sky.*

Thus is the essence of the teaching of the "Song of the Free," a view of the perception of a being which is consciously aware of the nondual nature of ultimate reality.

He attains the supreme, eternal Self who is not mind, intelligence, body, senses, or egoism. The avadhuta, alone, pure in evenness of feeling, abides happy in an empty dwelling place. Having renounced all, he moves about naked. He perceives the Absolute, the All, within himself. Know me to be That. There is not the least doubt about it. The avadhuta, having realized the truths of the scriptures, has uttered this spontaneously from his own nature.

That Ultimate Moment

I amused Katherine Holden, my valued assistant, when she said one day, "It appears to me that you must stay up late. What time do you go to bed?"

I said, "I always go to bed at midnight...actually, a minute or two after midnight—that way, I know I've lived until the 'next day'!"

After considering this, she said to me later that she thought it would be useful if I were to write about what it is like for a Self-realized person (at 79) to be living in what he expects could be the final days of his life. Her suggested title for such a monograph: A Moment After Midnight.

To do this, I'd need to situate the matter within a comprehensive framework.

With the advent of Self-realization, one has "died" to one's "personal" identity. While we still answer to our given name, and still use the personal pronoun "I" when practical, we are fully aware that our true nature is That, the immovable presence "which does not come and go," the timeless Being which experiences neither birth nor death.

It is our bodies, and "individual" identity which take form, within this ever-present reality that has no beginning or end. And it is within this ever-present reality that our bodies, and assumed "mind" and "self," cease to exist as what appear to be independent forms.

So, of this much, one is already clearly aware upon Self-realization: material forms, and all which they "embody," are impermanent; the only thing which is permanent, unmoving, is that which existed before the appearance of transient "identities," and will last after.

Thus one has already "foreseen" the death of the body of each "person," that person's "self," that person's "mind." Yet, one recognizes something "else" remains. What is the importance of this recognition to the Self-realized?

We are all given a hint of what it means to no longer exist as a "person" or a "self"—or even as a "body."

In our deepest stage of nightly sleep, self-awareness is absent; in fact even awareness of being, or having, a body is suspended. The empty awareness which is present, in that condition, is not even aware of the extent of the emptiness of that condition. Body, person, mind, identity: "gone"; the absence is not missed, nor is there even any desire for recurrence.

This is our foreshadowing of obliteration—not only "personally," but of all existence of which we have ever been aware. Our awareness in deep sleep is entirely empty of a world on this earth, as well as a universal cosmos in which any reality whatsoever exists. All gone.

This is our daily "reminder" of the status which is as death-like as death could possibly be: emptiness, without even an awareness of the totality of emptiness. Not anything left; not even an awareness that you—or even the universe—ever have been: no trace of any existence that was even a possibility, nor even imagined.

In the ultimate sense, then, how "meaningful," how "important" is any "reality," how seriously ought we to take our life: it is no more significant than a fleeting dream.

It is this awareness which is the conscious state of the thoroughly Self-realized. As a consequence, his attention is merely on the moment, as one is when witnessing the unfolding of a dream. His mind has emptied of substantial content, retaining only what is practical in terms of day-to-day living.

Wherever he looks, and whatever he views, he sees only impermanence: emptiness—recognizing that he who sees is no less empty. "His" life, the world, the universe can cease to be—even to ever have been—at any moment.

This recognition, this awareness, dictates his every movement—every one of which holds the amusing "importance" of potentially being his last. Therefore, since no moment bears any more importance than any other moment, it matters not to him when that ultimate moment will appear.

So, he has, in a sense, "died before one dies," and his absence, or non-existence, is as much in his conscious awareness as is his momentary presence.

This is to be free, and at peace. It is to transcend "the fear of death." There is only the Endless, for which there is no such reality as "time," in the moment after "midnight."

> Poised at the pond's edge
> the dew drop slips from the leaf
> stilling the Still pond.
> — Katherine Holden

Call Off the Search

Rachel:

The years you have spent in meditation have not been wasted: they have demonstrated to you that you cannot get where it is that you want to go *by effort*.

Why?

Because there is no *where* that you need to go.

You *are*—though you may doubt this—where you hope that you'll be!

When you want to know, firsthand, who *you* are—where do you *go* to do that?

Look. Truth *cannot* be hidden.

Focus on these comments from the monographs that aroused your attention:

"That essence—which is present in every iota of matter and energy—forms a singular, whole connection as the basic, common identity of all things.

"How much closer can Brahman, or Essence, be (which knows no distance) than to be yourself?

"Your capacity to recognize Intelligence is this Intelligence in recognition of itself. The Absolute, being all things (including you), anything which any aspect of it contemplates is It contemplating Itself.

"It's not that it is too mysterious or too sublime or too complex for words, but rather because it is too simple, too obvious, too close to be caught in the net of the subject–versus–object perspective."

How much simpler—and easier—can it be?

Enlightenment is nothing more than the profound realization "I am that."

Therefore—and this is the most fundamental aspect of the realization—there is not really an I in I Am That: there is *only* That.

The I—the self—dissolves when you recognize this truth: only the essential Presence remains real and this essential Presence is (must be) where you sit *now*, and where I sit now—always whole and unbroken everywhere.

This is not news to you. You've been hearing it for decades. (Intuitively, even, you know it to be true.) In Buddhism, upon awakening, an expression is often repeated: "Buddha and the 500 patriarchs have not lied to me!"

Why is it that we come to this truth so reluctantly? Because it tolls the death for the "self." It is a life-changing realization. And many people are not open to a change in their life that this change in perspective heralds.

Therefore, the "search" (subconsciously) continues.

But that *too* is seen to be okay, when you recognize that "you" are not the doer. *Whatever* is done, is That doing what it does!

So, whether you "realize" (or not) really makes no difference!—because you are inescapably that Presence, whether you are "aware" of it or not. Hence: search ended, as well.

Contemplate these matters!

Who to Believe?

Science tells us the earth is four and a half billion years old. Yet, hominids didn't appear till two *million* years ago.

Egypt was being settled, by early humans who had speech, about 700,000 B.C.

Not till about 70,000 B.C. did Neanderthal man arrive on the scene. And 43,000 B.C. saw the arrival of our species, Homo (whose life expectancy was less than 30 years). At least by 10,000 years ago, people were harvesting grain, hunting with bow and arrow, and cooking in clay pots. Around 5000 B.C., we were brewing beer.

Yet, by Newton's time (17th Century), you could read a footnote to the creation story in the Bible, asserting that God created the world in 4004 B.C. (on October 23, at 9 A.M., according to a church authority).

How the 'Story' Ends

Amun:

If you are a male, you know you are a male: you don't find yourself half of the time walking into the women's restroom.

Likewise, when you *know* that you are the ever present Self, rather than the manifest-form "self," you don't maintain that "I am *That*" when you're happy, and "I am *me*" when you're not.

To "abide (meaning; "go on being") as you *are*," for an awakened person, means to abide as the *Self*. Remaining as the *me* is not a "shift in perspective." The awakened person has *died* to the me: therein, the me's *past* and *future* also have no continuing relevance. What now survives is an impersonal witness: it doesn't identify with what it witnesses. For example, the witness does not identify with the person who is feeling sorry for himself. *It* is what is *aware* that someone is feeling sorry for himself. It doesn't identify with the person who is recalling his painful past. *It* is aware that someone is recalling his painful past.

The self-less witness, in the awakened, is not holding a part-time position with a terminal me. If the me hadn't thoroughly died, Self-awareness would not be there. The presence of Self-awareness is a consequence of knowing that there *is no me*.

It isn't Self-awareness which is, for example, feeling sorry for itself, or cursing its past.

When you know that you are the Absolute, as surely as you know that you are a male, whatever apparent "disturbances" arise will be witnessed without self-identification, passively. Goodbye to "Oh, woe is me!"

When a "personal" upset is experienced, you can't trace it back to the dispassionate witness. Look for a me who is not abiding continually in his true nature.

No whining, please.

Beyond Expectation

Robert:

This morning, walking in a little park, this insight came: "If everything is the Absolute, all this is the Absolute (meaning also, this is complete and perfect), there is nothing to search for, the search is over."

There was a release with it, but not something special. So the thought came (which is the Absolute too): "This can't be it, there is no deep sense of peace and love, a great sense of freedom, not even bliss." And I realized that this expectation was always there in the background, since the age of 22. Reinforced also by what some teachers say about awakening, about liberation in terms of an "energetic contraction releasing itself in boundlessness" (which seems quite dramatic), and so on.

So this expectation was always there, veiling the simple recognition of What Is, and resisting what is, creating in this sense a me!

And even if pain comes, or emotional suffering, this is it too.

Could it be so simple, or do I miss something?

Thank you, Robert, to be there with "me."

– Andre

You're not missing anything, Andre! It *is* that simple. "Not something special."

The spiritual literature leads us to expect (I can say from my own experience) a dramatic "event." But we have simply come to realize that there is no way in which the "me" can be "outside of" ultimate Reality.

When the "me" dissolves into this Truth, "there is nothing to search *for*, the search is over."

Harmonious Being

From the farthest star in the cosmos to the tiniest subatomic particle in your body, there is a universally-present Intelligence which holds in equilibrium and harmony every iota of existence, external and internal.

If you recognize that "you" cannot possibly be apart from this all-inclusive actuality, then you must also recognize that anything "other-than-you" is likewise imbued and affected.

This is not to say that one is to ignore that we have the capability of recognizing a particular named form, or entity, as compared to a dissimilar form: thus even the enlightened (such as Buddha or Ramana) occasion the relative terms "you" and "I," and answer to their name.

The point of the teachings of Oneness is to fully acknowledge in consciousness that there is an underlying interconnection in all of these forms of appearance, which supersedes seeming distinctiveness.

Yes, there is a "me" and a "you"; but to what source do all manifested things owe their common existence?

If this underlying nature of *Beingness* is not clear to you, not anything else which is said in the nondual teachings will ever make any sense to the seeker of jnana.

However, if the aforesaid is clear to you, then you can surely recognize that everything which these apparent forms act out owes its existence to the ubiquitous Intelligence which informs every aspect of Being—including *your* being, and *whatever* it is that you are manifestly being.

Your "loop of thoughts and feelings" and perception "I am not good enough" are not somehow magically left out of this universal development of expressed Beingness. IT does not act out in (what you consider to be) a purely positive way: positive and negative are in existential harmony.

You and all others are expressions of this Being—as is *all* that is *done*—whether you concede that this is so, or not.

Crucial

*Different spiritual teachers emphasize different things. I
find your clarity most helpful. What you would say are
the most important teachings for the seeker?*

As a consequence of my talks with scores of people, only
two points have proven to be crucial.

The seeker must comprehend (and when she does, the
seeking is definitely finished) that what is being sought,
the Absolute is not something which we eventually come
to encounter—because, due to its very nature, it is always
inescapable. All spiritual traditions refer to sacred, or
divine, Being as infinite, eternal, without limitation.
Obviously, such an actuality has to be present *where* and
when you are, regardless of your location in time and space.
The seeker cannot under any circumstances be apart from
what is sought.

The second element of the teachings, which instill the
awareness out of which we then live our lives in complete
Oneness, relates to the major question that arises: "If the
Absolute is present here now, why don't I feel it?"

Infinite, eternal, formless Beingness is present not only
where every form is, material or immaterial; it permeates all
that exists: "*Nowhere* is it not," as the Vedas put it. Your
very *Being* is whatever you happen to be *feeling, thinking,*
or *doing.* The infinite, eternal, unbounded Absolute is the
doer, the source, of all that is ever being done.

When this principle is clearly recognized, it is seen that
the Absolute is the fundamental, universal identity of all
that exists. In other words, as the Vedas state, you and

the Ultimate Reality are not two different things. This realization of Oneness is the ending of division—duality, as one's basic, conditioned perspective—and thus of conflict. Out of this Absolute awareness, then, one lives the balance of one's life; confusions about the nature of life and how to live it have been utterly clarified. What is regarded as the self is no longer viewed to be anything other than ultimate Being, present in material form.

Going Where "You" Will

From an embryo, a human body, brain, sense organs (and so on) are formed; a baby is born, and the baby grows through infancy. Somewhere—throughout the process of conception through adolescence—we would say that this human organism acquires "will" (which we generally regard as autonomous, intentional choice and action).

If we were to surmise that the bodily organism itself was a manifestation of the Void, or the "Ground," then we would likely surmise that the organism's subsequent "will" was also a manifestation of that self-same source. Many choose to refer to such a source in terms of "God." In any case, to accommodate this latter form of terminology, we could say this: when will *does* become manifest, it is—from this perspective—not by *our* will (that is, the organism *without* will) that it becomes manifest, it is by God's will. In this sense, it can be conceived that our will was God's will, "always has been" God's will.

Obviously, personal will and "consciousness," particularly "self" consciousness, are intertwined. And what can be said of the origination of will can be said of the origination of consciousness. And we would suppose, consciousness is intertwined with such manifestations as thought, imagination, belief, and memory. Typically, when conscious, we think and imagine; form beliefs; and we recall our images and beliefs through memory. It is such processes that appear to be at the *base* of our "will," of our intentioned personal choice and actions.

It seems, in general, that it is via this network of intertwined psychic phenomena—consciousness, thought, imagining, conviction, memory, will—that we set about to establish our personal "relationship" to the "things" of our world and to interact with them. It is, in fact, the same will (that is involved in the creative perception of our world) which eventually desires to impose *changes* among the relationships of some of the things of this world: our same will "creates" and our same will "destroys." In this, again, it could be supposed to be God's will.

All of the above elements of the network of the human psyche might serve a function; but (just as with the human body) these functions may be subject to change, to impermanence. It is evidently possible for memory, opinion, images, even thought to fall away, and for the body to continue functioning. Will, itself, and consciousness, may even fade away. There can come a time when even our most primal expression of will—the will to survive—dissolves. In this instance, where there is neither the will to live nor to die, we might say that our will is most like God's will: the Prime Mover need have no will concerning survival or nonsurvival.

At this point of our discontinuance, when our personal will (and personal consciousness) falls away, our will is—as it was and has always been—God's will.

Post Awakening

John:

For years, I have corresponded with an inmate who practically knows the Course in Miracles by heart. Like so many so-called "inspired" (or channeled) texts, its pronouncements are so ambiguous that a person can read into it any conclusion desired.

After a "dramatic spiritual shift," as you describe it, some people do feel a need for guidance concerning adjusting to this change in perspective

I haven't yet heard from anyone who says they've had a genuine nondual awakening solely through studying the Course (in fact, to the contrary). If you feel the need for further guidance, I suggest you locate a teacher of nonduality whom you conclude is truly Self-realized and, where possible, communicate directly.

Each person's post-awakening unfolding is unique, although there are common elements. Only the teachers who recognize this will be able to resolve your concerns. There are some who can.

Estrangement in Progress

Many people, today, go into their garage in the morning, drive to work, sit throughout the working day in front of a computer, and then return home again without one significant contact with another human being during the entire day. Even a withdrawal at the bank, on the way home, is simply another interaction with mechanical equipment.

And on a beautiful summer day, a child might spend the entire day in front of television, with no interaction with playmates or the tangible world.

This is not to say that isolation occurs only under such circumstances. One can remain equally isolated within a small circle of close friends or family or associates.

And in a metropolis, numbering millions of people, one tends to be aware that it is unlikely that *any* particular passer-by will ever be encountered again: there appears to be little incentive, therefore, to be of assistance to another person.

If it is true that we come to know ourselves through relationships and interactions with others, what does this say of our increasing, sterile isolation?

Unlike isolation, solitude doesn't disallow interrelationships. While solitude and isolation both have been, and continue to be, elements of human existence, it is isolation—and not solitude—which appears to be the predominant trend. The most saleable technology seems to be that which offers engineered escape from unmediated interaction with other—unpredictable and fallible—humans. As a comic once quipped: "I *love* humanity! It's *individuals* I can't stand."

Can we be aware of our innate capacity for the engagement of solitude (which basically can provide a movement toward freedom from attachment), and also of our tendency to yield to the impulse of isolation (which is primarily a reaction involving aversion or alienation)? There is a significant difference (as experiment will demonstrate) between risking an exploration of the unknown in solitude and, conversely, clinging to the fantasy of security in isolation.

Supreme Intelligence

To the "man on the street," it was an "intelligent" human who planted a flag in the barren soil of the moon and posed proudly by it, in the world's most expensive photo opportunity. Thus, we generally equate intelligence with a primate's ability to assemble mechanical parts, to methodically follow the schematic of linear thought and its projection of calculations.

A typical dictionary definition of intelligence might read, "ability to acquire and retain knowledge; mental capacity to solve problems; cleverness." A less self-conscious definition usually follows; "information, or news." At the bottom, there is sometimes an even less worldly definition: "an intelligent spirit or being."

Such definitions might lead one to wonder: is intelligence an extraneous ingredient, which could be dispensed with (similar to nutmeg in a cake mix) in the universe? In other words, where a brain (or a being) were enitrely absent in the cosmos, would the cosmos be operating then without intelligence? It is interesting that, in evolutionary terms, there was sexual reproduction for 370 million years before there were brains.

Put another way, can intelligence be apart from anything, or is intelligence—in its deepest meaning—simply another description for the all-pervasive and ever-present "essence"?

As a Johns Hopkins neurologist put it: "People think all intelligence resides in the brain, and therefore that if you take out half the brain, the patient ought to be half as intelligent."

An example was given of a girl whose entire left lobe of the brain (the "verbal" hemisphere) was removed at age twelve. Yet, "Shown a picture of a chair, Denise might say, 'sitting in it.' If we show her a picture of a bell, she might say, 'ringing it.'"

The relationship of intelligence to an organism's central nervous system is like a Constitution, which governs: did the Constitution create government, or was there prior governance which created the Constitution? Is intelligence the consequence of your ability to perceive, or vice versa?

That which sees through your eyes, saw through your eyes when you were a prehistoric primate, as well as when you were a primordial reptile: there was never a time when Intelligence did not see through your eyes—and the eyes of all others in existence.

This is the intrinsic property that physicist Fritjof Capra is referring to:

> Since motion and change are essential properties of things, the forces causing the motion are not *outside* the objects, as in the classical Greek view, but are an *intrinsic* property of matter. Correspondingly, the Eastern image of the Divine is not that of a ruler who directs the world from above, but of a principle that controls everything from within:
>
> 'He who, dwelling in all things,
>
> Yet is other than all things...
>
> Whose body all things are,
>
> Who controls all things from within...'

This is, as Krishnamurti alludes to it, that which in no way can be created by the mind of thought. "Whom all things do not know" because that which would be known is the knower. This essence, or intelligence, is no way external, conditional or causational. It is always ever present, therefore elusive to linear, limited thought: it is already present at any point which conclusions could reach. In other words, it does not depend on "rational intelligence" for its manifestation.

In the words of Joseph Needham, "harmonious co-operation of all beings arose, not from the orders of a superior authority...but from the...*internal dictates of their own nature.*" Put another way: no central intelligence agency; no "first principle" *before* this intelligence.

What this suggests, according to astrophysicist Paul Davies: "Inherent in nature (is) an absolute indeterminacy of the universe." No "ruler," as a repository of intelligence. The word for this self-genesis of all things is autopoiesis. Where there is this autogenesis, there is no need for anything to interfere, intercede or interdict with anything else. All trans-actions are harmonious, without effort and conflict, in this intelligent presence.

Generally speaking, human behavior concerns itself with reaction, inaction or action. And of the latter, there are two kinds: not all forms of activity, it must be obvious, are intelligent in the temporal context.

Reaction is predicated on some preceding, or past, action (thus "re", as in returning). In the historical metaphor, mankind's *first* reaction was Adam and Eve covering their ass.

Inaction, which is in the present, may be action sufficient to itself; it can also be the "void" out of which intelligent action precipitates.

Intelligent action, it could be said, is the action which expresses the Tao; put another way, action which is not dependent for its authority on calculative and consequential thought. Some would call this "self-less action."

The point of sagacious teachings is that man's energy is directed into reactive ideas, and ideals: *or,* into insightful behavior or presence (as action or inaction).

Unexplainable

When someone says,

"I'd know an enlightened person, if I see one,"

that's what's called "dry bones in the desert."

When someone says,

"I've chanted the Heart Sutra for sixteen years,"

that's known as "moss growing on the north side of the tree."

When someone asks,

"Why does the Gita say there's no such thing as time?",

that's what we call "a leaf falling into the creek."

When someone says, "There's nothing for me to surrender, since there's no 'me',"

that's what most say is "the breeze bending the grass."

When someone says, "I no longer argue with 'what is,' and I'm forever grateful for that!,"

this is what is meant by "rain on a parched field."

No-Fault Assurance

If there is anything which is timeless and formless, it has to be without cause. It is that which is without cause that, at the same time, sustains life and exterminates it.

The linear mind of man comprehends "dependence": *this*, he posits, causes *that*. He does not fully understand "interdependence": this cannot cause that, until that causes this. The former is a proposition dependent upon time; the latter is coincident or simultaneous, in which any causation would have to cancel itself out. Though we speak of "a cause" and "an effect," can you identify even one thing which has ever been caused by one other, single thing? Can you name anything which has ever been the effect of only one other thing?

Any cause which produced an effect would have "died" into the effect the moment the effect was "born." Put another way, since all present things depend on other present things for existence, there is not anything in the "past" which is solely causative for anything in the present.

The notion of temporal cause-and-effect is at the root of the idea that universal life is something which has been "planned" or ordered. At the bottom of this scheme is a central Planner who presumably exists in independence. Planning (and execution) is a process in time; the plans—and the Planner—would be dependent upon time. And any plan is a form, and all forms are subject to change. Any set plans of this (presumably infinite) Planner would be finite.

The beauty of the cosmos is that everything is okay, purely "because" there *is no plan.* No matter *what* happens, in this universe of random chance, it has *always* been *perfectly* okay. The miracle of this cosmos is that not *one* thing—*not one thing*—can go wrong. Now, is that beautiful—or what?

It is man's cunning to endlessly solve problems; it's the universe's intelligence to have never a problem. Man's dominion is one of constant control: the domain of the universe is one where everything competently, perfectly, manages itself: *everything*! Man views himself as "doer," at cause: the most common conceit is the boast that "I'm good at what I do!"

Buddha held up a flower, and most listeners concluded that this signified that something was to follow. But one listener understood that there is not anything in a position to follow; and his smile of response was immediate. No wonder that Buddha passed the flower over to him. One does not listen to a wind chime and inquire as to who composed the music.

No Justice

It is one of Ventura's two natural-foods restaurants, the Carrot something or other. This one is open after 7:00 p.m., and serves wine. It's outside of the strip which boasts the cute shops and the angled parking: facing it, across the street, is a Laundromat.

It has a deli case, an espresso bar, and tiled tables with plastic chairs. Watercolors adorn the walls and each has a price sticker.

I'm the only customer, and so the waiter lounges on a stool at the espresso bar, and chats with the owner.

The waiter is an energetic young man with a crew cut, wearing a black tee shirt under his green apron. The owner, who is methodically completing the pre-closing clean-up chores at the sink behind the bar, has graying, curly black hair and he wears glasses. The recorded music possibly dates him: Thelonious Monk; Joe Williams.

"Sorry I ducked out to my car for a minute," the waiter says, "but I had to call Kerry back. She just got home from work, and she buzzed me on the pager."

"Pager?!"

"You don't *hear* it. It just vibrates. I've had it since I was in high school—I was never at home to get my calls."

"Pager?!"

"Yeah. This one can reach you anywhere in the country. Satellite. She'd been out to the building site. 'My God, they've got the bathrooms stubbed in already?' Twenty four hundred square feet now: we decided to go ahead with the sunroom. Dad said we'd probably regret it if we didn't."

The owner, busily covering plastic containers in the deli case, appears to have heard none of this, yet he mutters, "Twenty four hundred square feet?!"

"How was lunch?" The waiter is peering though the glass into the deli case.

"Not too good. Sold four."

"As soon as we get moved in, you guys will have to come out and see our place!"

"Yeah. Say, could I get that pager number. You haven't been home sometimes when I've called you, and your machine answers, and it's a toll call for me."

"I'll put it on a post-it and stick it on the cash register." The waiter strips off his apron, dumps a pocketful of bills and change on the bar and counts it.

"Umm, not too bad. Eight twenty."

"Eight twenty?!"

Intelligence of Change

The "essence" of which we speak is not a property, which has a locus: being truly *essence-tial*, it is an actuality which is ubiquitous. Thus it automatically "governs" at each and every point that it happens to be—and it happens to be everywhere at once. Because it is everywhere at once, all "parts" of it are always constantly "in contact" with all other "parts" of it: that *is* the essence. And because of its omnipresent ("fundamental") nature, its governance—at *any* point, at *any* time—is sublimely intelligent. That all things, at all times and places, express "self-direction," or self-intelligence, is not only inevitable—under these circumstances—but wholly necessary.

The Latin root of the word *universe* means "all together," and the word is defined as "the totality of all things"; the (Greek) word *cosmos* is synonymous. Considering the universe, or cosmos, as all-inclusive, there could not logically be anything which stands outside of it or apart from it, which powers or propels the action or movement in this cosmos. In other words, the tendency for movement in all things lies within themselves. Any particular thing, and its movement, or perpetuation, are the *same* thing. Put another way, anything which could possibly fail to perpetuate its own form would succumb, and would die into another form which *is* perpetuating itself.

Our difficulty is to comprehend something which is wholly complete yet constantly changing, a perfection which includes the imperfection of unpredictability. We have difficulty understanding that imperfection is elemental to perfection, that perfection is not the eradication of imperfection.

*

"Take perfect from perfect,
the remainder is perfect."
—Upanishads

"States" and "Degrees"

When Shimano says, "There is no east, no west, no man, no woman," is he intimating that our relative conceptions are illusory?

So-called "realization" is a recognition that no such separate thing actually exists as "enlightenment" (and, conversely, "unenlightenment"). Therefore, realization is merely the recognition and ac*knowledge*ment that there is not any (separate) thing which can be *gotten*, or "*gained*."

So, when one has clearly "realized" this, the pursuit of enlightenment—or the notion of transcending from one "state" (or condition) to another—dissipates of its own volition.

The *idea* that there is any such *thing* as the "enlightened condition" or the "unenlightened condition" is a product of the human psyche: the nature of *thought* is *divisive*.

The nature of *seeing* (perceiving) is inclusive. The psyche has a nonlinear aspect, as well as the linear. It is possible to perceive in an intuitive, nonlinear recognition which preempts analytical, linear thought. This perception is *inclusive*, in the way that your eye takes in all within its range—until you *purposely* focus it on a particular object.

What is Ken Wilber saying about your "distance" from Absolute presence?

> "You *already* feel this…it is the…*present* feeling—no matter *what* it is that you suppose you're feeling! If you don't happen to *feel* you are enlightened, that is your *present feeling*."

Thus, when the definitional boundaries are removed (where they were formed, in the psyche), there is no actual "disconnection" between "states."

That presence (or event) that sages have referred to is that which remains when all names have been dismissed.

Then, it is not any *particular* thing. Yet, if you re-apply all the divisive names to its unlimited presence, it is also *all* of the things that have been *named*: man, woman, east, west, etc.

There cannot be, in other words, separate "states" (or conditions); there is but one overall, abiding condition (or state): that of the universally-present Absolute.

If you wish to point to some phenomenal aspect of the Absolute and appropriate a name for it ("man, woman"), freely do so. But if you lose "sight" of the Absolute nature of your relative conception, there is *confusion*.

Fixation

It's remarkable how much your thoughts about thoughts are concerning you.

Your consistent point seems to be that there are some thoughts which will somehow distance you from your true nature.

All that you do—and this includes thinking—*is* your true nature.

Your *true* nature is free of distinction: it is neither right nor wrong, good or bad. As a point of fact, it is not "true" or "false" either ("true," in the sense that it is referred to, is "basic," fundamental).

Since your (true) nature is your fundamental, *essential* nature, "you" are in no way *apart* from it: You *are* That.

When you do drop your concern that you are somehow divided from your true nature, you will cease to critique and classify your thoughts. ("Oh, no: there's that thought again, that takes me away from my true nature!")

You will instead merely witness, without judgment or anxiety, all the (previously-designated "good" and "bad") thoughts that pass unhindered, in and out, on the screen of consciousness.

How could any of these (free) thoughts have any impact or importance when there is no *value* attached to them?

When the sages say, "Do nothing," *critiquing* your thoughts is not "doing nothing."

Cosmic Consciousness

If you earned $100,000 one year, how many years would you need to match that in order to earn a billion dollars? Not ten years; not a hundred years; not a thousand years: rather, ten thousand years.

Viewed another way, take one step and think of it as 100,000 years. How far to walk to "a billion years"? About five miles.

Light travels at 186,000 miles per second. It takes about 1½ *hours* for light to travel a billion miles. In science magazines, you can view photos of galaxies whose light reached the camera lens after journeying 13 billion *years*.

In one year's time, light travels 5.88 trillion miles; multiply that by 13,000,000,000 years, and you have (at least) that many miles of the cosmos which we can see (not counting what we *can't* see).

And that's looking in one direction: look in the opposite direction, and the camera lens will there, also, intercept light that traveled 8½ billion years before our solar system even existed—and more than another four billion years before we were around to build that camera.

In this vast (if not infinite) universe, sits this earth—not even 7,500 miles wide, passed by light in a quarter of a second.

Contemplate such things, when you're evaluating your importance in the universe!

Upon Your Realization

Thank you for your well-written description of post-awakening developments. I'm always interested to hear such accounts: while there are general similarities in each unfolding, there are also unique aspects.

I've read your pages carefully. As you indicated, we are all thoroughly familiar with our customary conditioned—dualistic—perspective. But the emergence of "spiritual," or *nondual*, awareness—as if a "fourth dimension" were added—needs some getting accustomed to. Then, nondual awareness can become as natural as our dualistic perspective had always been.

You are noticing that—with nondual awareness—the relative, material world does not change in its appearance or eventualities: what changes is our "relationship" to such so-called realities.

The major change we notice is in our perception of the "viewer," of what is externally and internally observed. As dualistic demarcations are seen to be mere appearances, the "individual" himself is recognized to be insubstantial.

The sense of who or what our "self" *is* develops beyond the definitional limitations that have normally followed the words "I am..."

This freeing orientation cannot help but have an affect on both our values and behavior; thus we notice old self-centered patterns dissolving (without effort).

Whatever arises in consciousness, then, is merely inherent in the process of liberation from ego-preservation activities.

A new, creative energy can be released when our ideation of "should" and "should not" is lifted from our world-view.

No true awakenings, or their unfoldment, follow a pre-ordained format. As we empty out of self-identification, something fills that "vacuum"—and the lives of the Self-realized beings indicate that it can be trusted to be beneficent.

These predecessors welcomed their realization, and I know that you will too.

Reforming Patterns

The subliminal means of transmitting society's conditioning is through tradition. Tradition is the past, acting in the present. Our history books are reports on the conflicts, the abrasions, caused by tradition and the rigidity it encourages. In the same way that we are attached, by the investment we have made, in our own personal progress (dating back to the day when we were able to speak our first word), so are we attached to the "progress" represented by our collective history—even intangible progression of such things as customs, morals, ideals, culture. Pride and tradition are as milk is to cream.

The grid of society's rules meet and connect with each other, and each time a rule becomes outmoded and is abandoned, a new one takes its place in the arrangement. With no dramatic break in tradition, society is modified from generation to generation, but does not radically change; as long as tradition maintains, there is no traumatic threat to the security of the established, of the "old guard." (The *avant-garde* is simply the "new guard.") Even saints follow their own tradition, else they wouldn't be recognized by society as saints.

Morality divides. Morals are society's dictation of what will be accepted as normal behavior. *Normal* derives from "a rule," a yardstick, and refers to a measurement of an average, of conformity to the pattern. In determining, for example, whether our sexual activity is normal, we make a series of divisive choices: whether, first, to engage in sexual activity at all, or not; then, whether to limit that sexual activity to one sex gender or the other; whether to engage in it with one partner or more than one; and so on.

(In a subway station, I once was accosted by an attractive, but androgynous, hustler. Curious about the person under the makeup and ambiguous clothing, I asked, "Are you heterosexual, homosexual or bisexual?" The reply was, "Honey, I'm just *sexual*!")

An arbitrary line is an arbitrary line: we call the artificial division between California and Arizona a state "line," the division between California and Mexico a "border." Boundaries are intended to demark opposites, the opposition: I am here on the North side of the border, you are there on the South side. How is it that the line between California and Arizona *unites*—when within the confines of the United States—but the line between either of these states and Mexico *divides*? This is possible only when the people of California and Arizona *believe* themselves to be united, and when the people of California and Mexico *believe* themselves to not be united. Boundaries are created, and they can be dissolved. There is nothing which is eternal, immutable, about them.

That which the individual cultivates as the self, the collective cultivates as the nation. To observe the illusory force in abstraction, consider all that is proposed when one chants, "I pledge allegiance to the flag..." The concepts of family, church, state, each promote identity and isolation; there are people who are "special" (the ones who are in association with, who "relate" to, us) and people who aren't special.

If it is possible to be free of anger or greed, is it also possible to be free of obedience or loyalty? We associate war with anger; we associate peace with obedience. Is war independent of obedience (to ideals, if nothing else)? When anger has been suppressed, will peace be the result? One man's anger is another man's indignation. One man's obedience to law is another man's obedience to state. Are there imperfect ideals and perfect ideals? Or are there only ideals?

Where there is an ideal to kill for, and an ideal to die for, it is clearly only a matter of which side you are viewing that ideal from. When we have all psychologically died to ideals, who will march for war? And who will march for peace? If violence is a result of an idea, what is non-violence a result of? Can the reality of violence be invalidated by an effort in the opposite direction? Can't we face the fact that there is violence—inwardly and outwardly—and not turn away, to lose our attention in some ideal...treating it as subject/object, something that we have no involvement in perpetuating?

Aversion, avoidance, is a moving away—the creation of a space between, by choice. Resistance, opposition, rebellion, revolution, all establish their own traditions, authority and conditioning; the "new" which they bring is a *re*form, a modification or refinement, of the old. There are "new" ideals, new priorities, new titles, new costumes— new resolve to focus on becoming something different or "better" in the future. The most secure place to be is inside the matrix, the pattern; but a pattern is a form, and a form can change; and a reform can also change. To "reform" is to remake the old into a new shape, and that which has been reformed is subject to be formed again. Reform is the pendulum of the clock, causing the hour hand of history to "progress"—but never to cover ground that it hasn't covered before. The clock has had only one opportunity to sweep through entirely new territory.

We notice mechanical movement such as physical growth, and we speculate that there is the reality of psychological movement, such as spiritual growth or "raising our consciousness." Spiritual progress is viewed similarly to a joust with a pinball machine: when, with practiced control, the last light has been lit, the successful player is rewarded with the free game.

Can enlightenment be "obtained" in stages, like studying for one's doctorate, or climbing the Matterhorn...just a matter of desire and time, method? Can it simply be a matter of following a fixed, traditional pattern or practice?

Self-evident

"I follow your reasoning on the nature of omnipresence, that if there is an entity so attributed, then that entity is necessarily in everything and actually IS everything— but how do we prove the necessary existence of such an omnipresent entity?"

Originally, thoroughly acquainted with the *relative*, we go in search of the *Absolute*—only to discover that both are merely nominal aspects of the same indivisible actuality. So, even speaking of the "relative" and the "Absolute" are merely devices employed to get an illustrative grip on the one unbroken actuality.

But, then, we come to notice that even this nameless totality is beyond the pale of such limitations as "existent" or "nonexistent." That which the sage acknowledges to be without beginning or ending, and thus is formless, is no-thing, or empty or Void. You may prove or disprove the existence of *some thing*. What the thoroughly enlightened have awakened to is a condition wherein qualitative questions are not applicable to no-thing.

*

This Spirit, which is without beginning, is unborn and indestructible. It is not green or yellow, and has neither form nor appearance. It does not belong to the categories of things which exist or do not exist.

— Zen Master Huang Po

Forgetting the Mind

The question of thought-versus-no-thought, which you raise again, is really a non-issue—when perceived from the standpoint of nonduality. Your primary focus needs to be to answer *this* question to your own satisfaction: what is the ultimate nature, the truth, of actuality? When the answer to that question is unquestionably clear to you, the minor issue of "How is one to progress, from the present state of thought, to the desired state of no-thought?" will automatically resolve itself.

That which Wing-Shing Chan describes as "wunien" is awareness which is "empty of *objects* of the mind"; therefore it is also an awareness in which the *subject* is absent. You are the subject, the "thinker"; the objects in this case, are "thoughts" (including thoughts of *concern* about "thinking").

Hui Neng speaks (spoke) of "idea-less-ness," or freedom from "idle thoughts." All dualistic concepts are merely *ideas* about how the nondual actuality appears to be expressing itself. When the dual appearances have been resolved in your mind as the realization that—*whatever* you conceive— "That *too* is *It*," there is consequently only *one* thought, no "idle" thoughts.

Hui Neng describes further "an attitude of...no attachment, toward *all* things." That means not being attached to ideas of achieving some desirable condition, such as "no thought."

Chan elaborates on wunien:

"The mind does not fixate on *any* particular *instance* of thought... in any way that suffocates the free functioning of the mind...One does not hold a fixed *pre*-disposition...(wunien) is not the *termination* of the brain's thinking function."

Hui Neng is quoted on the enlightened mind: "When in use, it pervades everywhere." Chan adds, "Lucid awareness *and tranquility of mind* are wunien...*effortlessly* sustainable in daily life, it is enlightenment itself." The tranquility of mind is a consequence of having no "fixed predisposition"—such as a desire to *control* the mind.

Lucid *awareness*, permeated by *tranquility* of mind: "When the time is ripe...one realizes wunien [a mind unattached to either subject or object] and sees one's true nature." That does not mean to conceive of oneself as the "thinker" of "thoughts" (or the *non*-thinker of *no* thoughts.)

"In wunien, *thoughts arise* but do not attach to any external [or internal] objects..." The wooden spoon is so composed as to hold any manner of things as its content; its purpose is to allow everything to be emptied out, and to be perpetually empty for its next function.

Chan leads to the conclusion that he is referring to a presence in which "the mind *switches* from dualistic to non-dualistic perception, with no boundary and no opposition." (Thought-versus-no-thought: opposition.)

This is where, he says, one "appreciates the inconceivable, *simultaneous* existence of...universal *unification* of all things. A person (at this stage) can use thoughts *however* they please; discursive thoughts will not...cause *disturbance*."

In fact, he points out (as if it were a footnote), when one has "advanced" to a true emptiness of conceptual objectification, one "goes an extra step by...*forgetting* the mind"; it is now "effortlessly maintained...(with) *no mind* watching." The watcher and the watched have disappeared.

You remark, "I have been involved, caught up, in thinking... lost in duality." The watcher and the watched are in no way divisible. The "I" and the "thinking" *are* the "simultaneous existence of the universal unification of all things." Your left eye and your right eye see one thing.

Your "true nature" is your *present* condition, at this very moment—whether you are thinking or not thinking! There is only *one* "true" nature, that which is the *actual* fact—which is *always* here and now.

Discovering the Source

Ken:

The Thompson excerpt demonstrates something: it is possible to express the relative point of view; it is possible to express the Absolute point of view (to the extent that this can remain a possibility); to those who do not comprehend the difference (or even that there *is* a difference), this can create immense confusion!

For this reason (more than any other, I surmise) Maharshi, Ramesh, Krishnamurti and other prominent teachers are persistently misunderstood. If you speak strictly from the Absolute viewpoint (which some have done), how do you generate a dialogue with someone who (as yet) conceives only the relative viewpoint? However, when you initiate the dialogue by speaking from (or of) the relative (as Krishnamurti invariably did), how are they to recognize when you've shifted to the nonrelative viewpoint? A person to whom *both* contexts are thoroughly *clear* will recognize such shifts from one perspective to another. But these are not the ones who sit at the gurus' feet.

Ramesh is probably the most misunderstood teacher of Advaita today. Anyone reading his writings from the nondual perspective can follow clearly what he's expressing. If you stop a man on the street (or woman, either) and ask: "How would you define 'the Absolute'?", he'll stare at you blankly. But ask, "How would you define 'God'?"...

So, Ramesh (and others) use, for example, the word God as a synonym for what *they* perceive as the *Absolute*. No teacher of Advaita would assert that you are apart from the Absolute; but "everyone knows" that "you are not

God." So, one allusion refers to something which you automatically *are*, and the other to something which you (automatically) are presumed "*are not*." In the eyes of the Absolute, there's no such thing as subject and object; but in your eyes, you are "just one of God's subjects" (worshipping God as a distant object).

Thompson suffered such confusion with Balsekar. However, he understood enough from Balsekar that when he turned to the writings of Shankara (who refused to speak from anything but the Absolute perspective), he seems apparently to have fathomed his misunderstanding.

The area where most people misapprehend Balsekar has to do with non-doership. To put this in "layman's" (relative viewpoint) terms, he refers to God's will. But this assumes that you have already inculcated the understanding that *you are* God. "Your" will is "God's" will; and vice versa. It also assumes that you understand that "will" is a relative concept—in the same way that "you" and "God" are merely referential terms the sage uses to try to awaken the seeker to his true nature. So, for those who've skipped over the math, they stumble on the algebra. Not having paid attention in class and done their own homework, they walk away from Ramesh talking about "destiny" and the "pre-programmed"; they missed the part about the Absolute being void of time or intent.

Fortunately (for someone who's willing to forge through Shankara), there are some teachers who make no attempt to build a bridge for the spiritual recalcitrant. Shankara put Advaita on the map; others, like Ramana and Ramesh, built highways. Put another way, you can get your Advaita from someone like Ramana or from someone like Shankara. Thompson got started by Balsekar and moved on to

Shankara. What he says, as a result of his study, is not anything Balsekar would be in disagreement with:

"In the instant of (Realization)...all differentiation ceases. There is no separated seeker, divided from what is sought. ...the seeker disappears... no free will, no pre-destination..."
[So what's become, now, of "*God's* will" and "*my* destiny"?!]

"...what we really *are* transcends...'me' and God, both of which...never existed. Advaita wants the seeker to realize just who or what he really is. And that realization can only be object-less... what he seeks is what he really is. [God?!]...self-realization means simply returning to one's own true nature, which is the unaffected source... all our experiences express that...all expressions of caring—or not caring—are superfluous."
[So: what if it's "God's *will*" or my "*destiny*" to care?]

Evidently, Thompson got Balsekar's message—because Shankara's message is Balsekar's message, when they weren't *bothering* to build bridges.

Thompson's discoveries (as quoted above) are not dissimilar from the quotations of Nisargadatta:

"When you understand that names (are) without any content...you will be...in the deep silence of reality."
[nondual "no mind"]

"Abandon all conceptualization...and objectivization... identity cannot remain; and in the absence of identity there is no bondage."

Consider the idea *you* mentioned: "stay in touch with the undifferentiated Ground while going about daily life."

If this Ground is undifferentiated, it has no boundaries; therefore it is illimitable, ubiquitous: there's no-where that it's not. How could you be *apart* from it? If you can't be apart from it, how could you get (or stay) in touch with it? The Ground and your daily life are in no way separate.

Or consider your second idea:

When "the mind is very still, very quiet: *then* we are in touch with the Unknown...and we do not attempt to know it..."

There are no prerequisites (requirements) for being in touch with the Unknown (or Ground), since there's no prospect of *escaping* it. "Then" has no relevance to that which is eternally (timelessly) present. "You" and the "Unknown" are not separable, *whatever* state your mind (or no mind) happens to be in; *even* when your state of mind is that you are separate from the Unknown, that is the Unknown doing one of the myriad deeds that it does—along with 'living', 'dying', 'breathing', 'not breathing', etc. (Hence: "You are not the doer.") When your state of mind is that you *are one* with the Unknown, that too is another of the myriad thought-forms of the Unknown: it's all the same, one thing—just another expression or manifestation of the Absolute. Nothing special.

See again how thought divisively isolates "forms" through concepts?: I "do not attempt to know it" (the Unknown). If there really was an isolated, independent entity conceived as "I" and an independent object described as the Unknown, it could be possible for the subject (I) to relate to the object (U.)—to *know* it or *not know* it. If I and U. happen to in truth be the same, one thing, what "part" is there to "attempt" to know the other part?

Ramesh: "The one who is seeking is already what he is seeking..."

Thompson: "There is no separated seeker, divided from what is sought."

Nisargadatta: "...in the absence of identity, there is no bondage..."

I'm enclosing a copy of the Hsin Hsin Ming that you might want to contemplate, from my book *One Essence*.

Have No Fear

If the nature of *life* itself is a puzzle, surely the most difficult matter for us to conceive is the state of death.

The sense of being I, a person, will have vanished along with the mind and thoughts of consciousness, which have established and embedded it. There will be absolutely no thing to know, or be known, and no longer a knower to even know that.

So, our tendency is to imagine some thing form-less, which in some space, however empty, is in existence. But in the nothingness which obliteration in death represents, there is complete absence of things, including any thing which could exist as formless. Where there is no thing, nothingness, there is no *space* in which some post-life could remain; nor any *time* in which it could do so.

This is recognizable even as we are alive: in actuality, space and time are falsities even to those of us who are conscious. In fact the truth, greater still, is that we do not even *presently* exist as a person or a thing.

It is difficult for us to realize, or even to imagine, life and death are the same condition; see, there is no time or space which exists *between* them. But even the 'life' that we 'know', when we recognize that there is no reality to time and space, is a fiction.

Any thoughts that we have about either life *or* death concern the I—which is, and was, and will be nothing, non-existent: empty, void, completely.

Spirit-uality

No, I needn't complete what you've said "in its correct form." What you are expressing is well said, at length. Perhaps it will satisfy you if I restate it in my own words. I'll try to, generally, follow your outline.

First, let me say that the word *spirit* can be misleading in its use. My dictionary has a column of meanings three inches long. It is sometimes a synonym for a Jehovah-like God-figure; it is thought of as "*apart* from matter," especially the body; and sometimes conjures an image of a ghost (a separate entity).

The word *soul* is similar (two inches in my dictionary), considered to be "*part* of a person," which (at death) "goes somewhere."

Because of the distinctively separative nature of these words, their use can be unnecessarily confusing in a *non-dual* context.

However, I take your use of these words to be indicative of what I would refer to as "omnipresence," the eternally infinite actuality (which I generally call the Absolute). So, I'll try to retain the word you used, Spirit.

In speaking of the manifestation of "Spirit into form," I would tend to speak of it rather, Spirit *as* form. This helps to clarify that Spirit (always) is form; form (always) *is* Spirit; these have always been one actuality, never separate. It is in *Genesis* that Spirit precedes form, rather than is "coexistent" *as* form: the *Creator* and *created* are apart from each other initially, in the Biblical tale.

As you've said, the *formless* aspect of this actuality (Spirit) is unchanging: eternal, thus permanent. (The process of change itself is a form, in the *relative* arena of time and space.) And every aspect of *form* is changeable (and thus impermanent). As you put it, Spirit *"being* all, there is nothing that it *could* change *into."* (Thus, not Spirit *into* form.)

Most people think of "creation" as a completed act (some, "in six days"). But what is continuing-to-be-reality is a crea*tive* activity; the manifestation of formlessness as form (or, the Absolute as the relative) is an on-going activity— "eternally," as you wrote; and Spirit "is the only active principle." Spirit and activity itself, in fact, are the *same.*

At the core of all spiritual disciplines it is said that Spirit (Absolute) is omni-present, omni-potent, omniscient. *Being* All that is—in every place at every time, permeating every thing (material or immaterial)—it is ever-*present*, *all*-powerful, and *knower*/known of all. As you said, it is *all*-knowing because it is Self-knowing: all "knowing" forms are *its* form ("Self-conscious forms," as you put it).

It is not that forms are "subject to its will," it is that whatever *wills* (and consequently what is *willed*) is It, in its manifest activity. There is no thing that is subject to it (it not being an object); it *is* the *subject* ("condition") of all things.

This then brings us to your (poetic) expression: "The Spirit is conscious of its own thought, its own desires, its own manifestation of action; it's conscious of that which is manifest..."—because it *is* the manifestation of all that *could* be conscious; and is *even* consciousness itself.

"But it's not conscious of any effort, or progress, in its manifestation." As you've indicated, the formless is not of itself concerned with such ideas as *effort* or *progress* (being all-powerful, what relevance would that have?)— except to the (relative) extent that it is the *essence* of the *forms* which are concerned so.

You continue, "It's necessary that soul and body should exist because Spirit, without manifestation, could construct only a dream world—never resulting in Self-realization."

"Soul" and "body" (et al) are expressions of the formless; without conscious forms, there could be no such (reflective) reality as Self-realization.

The point of the non-dual realization, of course, is that "Spirit," "soul" and (intelligent) "body" are not three separate things, but one (Absolute) actuality. Buddhists have chanted for centuries: "Form *is* formlessness, formlessness *is* form." No contradiction there, where there is non-dual clarity (so-called enlightenment, Buddha's *real*-ization).

As you've noted, this is really self-evident; it is intuit-able, realize-able. You've been contemplating these matters (many hours a day?) and comprehending them.

Gandhi's Lament

I read, some years ago, Gandhi's autobiography. He states, there:

> "What I want to achieve—what I've been striving and pining to achieve these thirty years—is self-realization, to see God face-to-face, to attain *moksha*. I live and move and have my being in pursuit of this goal. All that I do by way of speaking and writing, and all my ventures in the political field, are directed to this same end...

> "Often in my progress, I have had faint glimpses of the Absolute Truth, God; and daily the conviction is growing upon me that He alone is real and all else is *unreal*....

> "I have not yet found Him, but I am seeking after Him. I am prepared to sacrifice the things dearest to me in pursuit of this quest. Even if the sacrifice demanded be my very life, I hope I may be prepared to give it. But as long as I have not realized this *Absolute* Truth, so long must I hold by the *relative* truth as I have conceived it."

Gandhi achieved universal honor for his pacifist political activities. While he was willing to sacrifice his "very life"— and, indeed, did—for that noble pursuit, he evidently was not willing to "sacrifice the things dearest to me in pursuit of this quest" for Self-realization. The thing dearest to him was self-rule for India.

Although he said the Absolute "alone is real and all else is unreal," his was a pursuit of a—however benevolent—worldly ideal.

To discover the Indivisible, one's priorities are best not divided by holding to the "relative truth" while aware throughout that this is ultimately *unreal*.

Being What Is Sensed

The enigma that you're trying to fathom is one of the fundamental paradoxes of Advaita. It is, in a sense, counter-intuitive; so—as they say—it cannot be approached by the logic of the mind, alone.

One must *begin* with the recognition that the definition of the Absolute is that it is *all-inclusive*.

Therefore, by its nature, it is the *observer*, the *observing* and the *observed*. For the sake of *linguistic* communication, we break it up into categories based on their seemingly-different *appearances*: subject/verb/object; "I" (That) "love" (That) "you" (That). "All that *is*," is taking the form of "I," the form of "loving," and the form of "you."

Leo, then, is presenting you with some examples of this phenomena, though (you will notice) it is a very subtle point.

For instance, his example where "knowing" is the activity. "You"—as the Absolute—cannot know of anything which is *not* (also) the Absolute. So, when "you" are aware of the Absolute, it is only the Absolute being aware of *itself*.

This is why the "illusory me" (as you put it) does *not* know that there "is no 'me'." What *does* know that there is no 'me' (*because* what we *consider* to be the 'me' is actually the Absolute) is no longer *imagined* to *be* the 'me' (because the 'me' *dissolves* into the Absolute, when its *recognized* that the Absolute is the essence of *all* that is).

So, the 'me' does not have an "experience" of knowing the Absolute. It is only when the 'me' is realized to *be* the Absolute that the Absolute will then be known.

You need to contemplate this conundrum, so that this fundamental aspect of *non*-duality is thoroughly clear in present awareness. It cannot, otherwise, be presented in a linear-logical manner.

Let go of the idea that yours (or any "other") is a *separate form*—and see what develops.

That Feeling of Unity

We compare the 'what is' with the "what could be," and we desire to escape into the "what could be."

We "could" feel a sense of unity with all things—but we don't, and that is 'what is.' If we can remain with that feeling of disunity, fully abide with it, what becomes of that disunity? When "disunity" is no longer held out at arm's length as something which is preferably *apart* from "oneself"—as an undesirable object which is regarded by the dissatisfied subject—there is a complete unity with it. When there is complete unity between the observer and that which is observed, such things cease to exist as an entity of concern. And in the absence of disunity, unity is all that can remain.

To give attention to the 'what is'—the feeling of disunity—is to cease comparing the 'what is' with the "what could be." Where there is no comparison, we face and deal with the actuality; there is no continuity of the "problem." The divisive desires of the self evaporate in the light of direct attention.

There is not anything to be gained in the feeling of a "state" of unity. For the feeling of a particular state of unity to be maintained, continuously, it would necessarily need to be maintained within the separate consciousness of the self. Any recognition of such a state would be as the result of a memorable comparison.

The desire to seek and achieve a sense, or feeling, of unity can be traced to the self's desire for "transcendent" experience. The self desires to possess a transcendent "experience," without itself risking total unification *in* transcendence. The idea that the *self* can attain (and maintain) transcendent unity is a gaining idea. In that which, by definition, lifts one to a state beyond comparison—completely transcendent unity—there could be nothing to gain. Unity can never be anything more than a state of comparison, and comparison is the specialty of the fragmented self.

Instantaneous

Robert:

While half asleep, and half awake, it was like Alice dropping into the rabbit hole; a portal opened somewhere within, an opening into Infinity: a total freedom of being absolutely nothing, merging into everything —the vast fathomless Beyond.

Now it is understood; this tenuous and ephemeral "cord" which connects us to a physical body. Oh, the joy, when it's recognized there's no need to return—to live fully each moment, yet die to the individual "me" ... before one dies physically. This is the Way. Boundless gratitude.

– No longer a "pilgrim"

Keep the Change

Habits are the pattern of memories, and the "past" is an excuse for our behavior in the "present," both individually and collectively. The bond between "individual" and "society" is conditioning, tradition. The only proximity to "unity," in our world, is in the sense of separateness which we commonly appear to *share*—our typical selfishness. We have shattered the vessel of the truth of wholeness, and we wonder why our lives seem barren and scattered. Not only in our materialism, but in our loneliness, our deep insecurity is reflected; and yet we are so mired in our patterns that we continue to stagnate.

Our abiding problem is that we chronically desire something other than what exists in this present—the only real—moment; we typically wish continually for that which is not being given by our circumstances. Though the predictable is static and lifeless, we suppose that that is what we want. But the Dance of Shiva does not confine itself to one posture. It is the chaos in the mixing bowl which produces the cake.

Only when we can harmonize with the present, critical situation is there any prospect that we will be able to harmonize with a change to a different status. We cannot expect to be an unmoving fixture in a reality which we hope will be vibrant and dynamic. We waste our energy in concerned anticipation, rather than assuming that nature knows what it's doing. In each appearance of every *thing*, we fretfully note "differences," and thus we conceive "problems": these problems are not unrelated to our conceptions. To the extent that we conceptualize, we will un-earth problems.

Change is a natural "perspective restorer." But man is so resistant to fundamental change that it seems probable he would resist heaven on earth, were it magically to appear. The most astonishing change we could make would be to live as one with the changing 'what is', rather than endlessly attempting to construct 'what should be'. The 'what is' is actual, not ideal; it is perfect in its chaotic imperfection; and attempt to control it is superfluous. When you strain, constrain or refrain, ask yourself why. Let us at least stop wasting energy on justifying and rationalizing our misguided behavior. There is more to life than hammering at a nail.

Resistance is the first impulse in the desire to control change—but change is irresistible, so we can only *try* to control change. Escape is the final impulse in the attempt to control change, but escape is merely postponement in time. To idealize is the impulse to imagine change that is under our control; chaos, however creative, is not thought of as ideal. (According to White's Law: Things are never as bad as they turn out to be.)

The seeds of control are in the fruit of fear. Observe that zenith of control in the West, "organized" (allopathic) medicine. Invasive, compulsive coercion of the body's physical systems has not allayed our dread of cancer. Contrivance does not dissuade nature. Left to itself, disorder finds its own order, inevitably; that's why chaos can persist. Nature need not worry about "setting an example"; flexibility could not be more natural: that which is controlled requires further control, and nature has no energy to waste.

It is fear of insecurity that dictates man's activity. We aspire unceasingly to bring to the present the security of a dead past or an imagined, idealized future. "Though we will not kill a cow to save our lives," an Indian swami said, "we will kill other humans to save our country." The tendency of our species is to say, "When I have my physical needs taken care of, I will care for spiritual needs." Yet, among those who have done the former, they are not particularly inclined to do the latter. The equation, apparently, is this: the more things you possess, the more fears you have. Security is its own reward. The further that one opens the jaw of security, the harder the bite of insecurity. There is complete freedom only when you can say, "There is not anything which you can take away from me." That is to give up everything without being lessened. To *clarify* is "to clear"; to *clear* is to "take away." There is something which is freed when you let go. Though a baby learns first to take a hold, this is followed by learning to release.

Desire is not really the problem; it is attachment to desire which is the problem. The most fundamental change possible for us is to let go of desire. When you can rest somewhere without desiring anything, as Buddha realized, you will have no problems.

Attachment is a connection which binds. First comes desire, then attachment, dependence, instability. First comes, for example, desire to excel; then attachment to results, dependence on competition, and instability of relationships—creating a *new* desire, for harmony. Take inventory: what is it that you desire not to lose?; then consider what you will do to *maintain* it. Confront potential lack of security and you confront fear. There is no guarantee to life, liberty and the pursuit of happiness. The *most* secure animal is in a cage.

To make an investment in anything is to expect. Expectation fathers worry. If you insist on expecting anything, expect uncertainty. The greatest bounty is there for who least desires it: having no expectations, there is perpetual abundance. Attached to outcome, one's actions can have only one direction: flexibility is lost. A mirror which held onto past images would soon be clouded and useless. A *temple* for "Truth" would be its tomb.

What is the connection between peace and non-attachment? Is our task to mold the world into a better place, a safer place, a more comfortable or predictable place—any kind of place but the place it happens to be as we encounter it? Is our deepest greed our greed for certainty? Is it not our "progress" which increasingly engenders fear of the future?

To simplify one's life means to do more than lease the house and retire to a Winnebago. What of our attachment to pleasure, entertainment, experiences, fulfillment—all transitory, all hollow? One can be earthy without being worldly. Generally our attitude is toward generosity and sharing: to whatever extent the *actions* in your life are not based on it, such *concerns* are merely theoretical to you. If the "perennial teachings" are not simply to be discarded as impractical, how do we manifest them in practice? When the obstacles to love are dismantled, there is no barrier to loving.

On The Timeless Trail

In the Ten Ox-herding Pictures, familiar to the student of Zen (found in such books as Phillip Kapleau's *The Three Pillars of Zen*), a series of framed aspects in the life of the enlightened are depicted, beginning with a young man in search of an "ox" (enlightenment), and ending with an old man who has no concern for any particular worldly thing, including ox or self ("The gate to his cottage is shut, and even the wisest cannot find him").

When first we examine these pictures, with our conditioned eye, we view them in linear fashion: the old man's "past" at the beginning, on the left side; the youth's "future" on the right side, leading to a conclusion. Our normal impulse is to consider the advent of enlightenment as a course over a period of time.

Were you to have no concept of time (beyond that of a particular interlude which we define as a "moment"), you could shuffle these ten pictures and you would recognize that a *bodhi* might conceive himself in any one of the frames, from any given moment to the next: the wise old man this morning, the ignorant boy this evening. When we have erased the time tracks from the page, the beginning is the ending, and the ending is just the beginning. There is no anchorage for the ship which remains under sail; there is no end to learning; the cottage gate that closes can open.

With your cognition of time freed from bondage, it will also be apparent to you that, were the frames translucent and stacked upon each other, there is but one time and we are each the full expression of it in our every action.

You are the old man *and* the young boy, and you were never in any way separate from each other.

Life and Death Matter

There is, it is apparent, no issue which is more central to our life than our death. It is an inescapable transition from the known to the unknown. As Shakespeare said, "We fear what we know nothing of." It is in that which is known to us that we identify "security"; it is in that which is unknown to us that we identify "insecurity."

Conditioned, as we each have been from infancy, to view the world of "reality" in subject-object duality (me/you; us/them; we/it; this/that; pleasure/pain; like/dislike; heaven/hell; life/death; here/there; now/then; beginning/ending; cause/effect; unity/multiplicity; form/formless), death is viewed as a singular event, as a form or condition, which is opposed to life. Polarized as it is, death is considered to be a separation *from* life; the "self," which presumed to be united with the living, is "separated" from the living in—"by"—death. Clearly, this can be a true proposition only if death is some thing which is, in actuality, separate (or divisible) from life. But there is not death which exists *independently* of life; there is an inseparable phenomenon, in which the very fact of one's existence owes its reality to the fact of one's potential nonexistence.

So if, on the other hand of possibility, the existence of a "condition" called life is interdependent upon a "condition" called death (and vice versa) the true nature, or identity, of these "conditions" is the same.

With all that we define as death in this world (the last breath), that which we define as life (the first breath) is continually unceasing: death has not ended for man, life has not ended for man. We would likewise say that when life ends for man, death ends for man: life and death are inseparable.

If, as is being suggested, life and death cannot be polarized ("disunited"), does that not—in like manner—apply to others of our supposed polarities? Are you truly a separate, isolated subject in a world of unrelated, independent objects? If you and every other human being are dependent (as you *are*) upon the same basic conditions for survival—food, for instance—you are all *inter*dependent. If there is no food for any human in the world, the result is the same for "you" as for "them."

Just because each human is "different" doesn't mean that humanity is "divided." The confusion between difference and division is an aberration in the mind of man. Life and death can be characterized as different conditions, without concluding that they are divisible. The sky is filled with different clouds but they are interdependent upon the same condition.

Though we need not be the victim of divisive thinking, we will always be cognizant of differences—as long as we identify each "thing" or "event" by a particular, or separate, name. As soon as we declare, for example, that something has "form," we imply that there is some other thing which does not have form. And each form which we define by a separate name becomes a "different" form: *steam* is hot water, *ice* is cold water, both are water.

We say there is *life*, and we go beyond that to say that life has different forms: plant, animal, me, you. But—being a form—we (conveniently) tend to forget that "form" is, by definition, at one end of a (supposed) polarity, the other segment of which is "formless."

Put another way, the condition of form is dependent upon impermanence. Were it not for impermanence (whose manifestation we call change), all form would remain frozen as it is: if all human forms remained eternally unchanged in their present condition, both "death" and "life" would be empty of meaning.

Any thing which man identifies is merely a form ("me"). All forms come and go. And, so far as we can ascertain, the coming and going (change) is end-less.

All that *is* or *is not* is "actuality." Anything which we can identify as living or dead is actuality. Given that there is no distinction, no exclusive value, assigned to life over death— by that which transcends all separative distinctions—how then is the dead different from the living? Are not *both* forms of the same actuality?

Is the "self" not a form? (Even an *idea* of the self is a form.) The body is not permanent; is the "self" permanent? If the self survives after death, and all things change, what would the self change to?

If the self is impermanent, what is maintaining its separate form right now? Thought? Memories? Suppositions? Illusion? And could these be subject to change?

Death is the release, the relinquishing of form: the form of the body, the form of the self. The whole of life culminates in this movement. This is a moment of inescapable transition, of trans-form-ation.

If there were any way that you could assist someone in the transition of life, it would be to help them let go...to freely let go of all the "things" and "events" they had realistically or unrealistically considered themselves attached to, that they considered "theirs."

In contemplating our own death, that is what we will do. Sooner or later, we will relinquish our attachment to each and *every* thing or event—past, present or future.

Death is, by any measure, the central fact of our life. The letting go—whether we *yield* to change or *resist* it—is the inexorable movement that is common to each and every life. And we need not wait, until we have no choice, to "unify" or align our existence with the nature of that which transcends permanence. We can, any of us, die now in each moment, by relinquishing our attachments—particularly our subjective attachment to a sense of an objective "self." We *can* come to know now our true identity—as impermanence.

At a deathbed, Krishnamurti held the hand of a friend who said, "I'm dying." He replied, "And I'm dying with you."

Taking It All In

F.S.C. Northrup's reference to "the undifferentiated continuum" and "the differentiated continuum" suggests that these continuums meet seamlessly at their fulcrum, balancing each other out metaphorically. In its implied relationship to awareness in the human psyche, the undifferentiated aspect would seem to be equivalent to what Eastern mystics, such as Huang Po specifically, term "original mind"—awareness (as per the definition sometimes given of *rigpa*, in Dzochen) "which existed before we saw ourselves as a self"; that would be pre-egoic, to the extent that "ego" is a conscious construct of one's psyche. Therefore, since thought patterns are the framework of the egoic construction, rigpa is sometimes also described comparatively as "awareness free of distorting thought patterns."

From the standpoint of Northrup's terminology, the differentiated continuum represents the end (of the spectrum) which is not free of confused thinking. In a simplification, one might speak of a scale, with "absolute awareness" at one end, and "relative awareness" a component interfacing that.

"Relative awareness" is more readily understood by most people, since it is the "state of mind" which the "individual person" identifies oneself with (and by). This cognition recognizes each form encountered as separate in its context: the "I" against the backdrop of the universe. From here, as the Buddhists suggest, Samsara arises.

This is the dualistic mind, which places value on the antagonistic polarities of such contentious images as "good" versus "bad," "right or wrong," "us and them," etc. Ergo: "These are *my* thoughts. Some of my thoughts are *good*. Some of my thoughts are *bad*. I must *retain* the good thoughts and *dispose* of the bad thoughts."

This is a mind which limits its purview to isolated forms, each of which exists in relationship to some contrasting others. Due to the habitual separativeness of its thought patterns, it is restrained from gravitating across the continuum to its potential freedom in Absolute awareness; or the presence of the condition which *rigpa* implies.

Rigpa being difficult to elucidate, the Dalai Lama speaks of a non-dualistic meditation "where the mind is returned to a primordial ["original"] and natural state...(where) there is no sense of subject and object": such as 'me' and my 'bad thoughts.'

With the severing of the limitation of separative identifications, such as *me* and *thoughts*, "there is no attachment, or agitation at having these 'reflections' in your mind...You are not pre-occupied by what arises in the mind, nor does it cause you any distress."

This "fundamental innate mind of clear light...is an *ever-abiding* continuum of mind, which is inherent within us."

Absolute awareness is not some phenomenon which we are apart from. Put another way, with the word *continuum* in mind, we could state: "The Absolute mind is the Buddha mind. The relative mind is the Buddha mind." The Absolute mind, operating without *limitation* of form, has unhindered access to the relative mind. The relative mind, though not disconnected from Absolute awareness, is *limited* in *its* access, because of its attachment to the either-or polarities.

The *entire* continuum is inherent within us: the differentiated aspect is all-too *familiar* to us; the undifferentiated aspect is *potentially* also familiar to us—once the limiting tether of self-imposed separativeness is severed. At that point, one's awareness is free to move *along* the continuum to be present in the Absolute and/or relative reality, as circumstances dictate.

In plain terms, the presence of non-dual awareness does not shackle the seer to an inert, vegetative stupor; nor does the presence of relative awareness consign the seer to an unrelieved future of petty concerns. His *normative* condition is one of unrestrained awareness, restrained when and where necessary to engage *specific* conditions. Rigpa is our "natural state": "The fundamental innate mind of clear light," says the Dalai Lama, "is considered to be the nature of mind, or the ultimate root of consciousness....

> "Yet it is not some unconscious state where you do not know anything, or never think of anything at all.... When this aware aspect of clear-light rigpa is directly introduced and recognized, it can be identified even in the very thick of arising thoughts."

So, the *thought* arises, "This is a bad thought. I must remove it!" And the *awareness* is, "This *too* is the Buddha mind!"

*

"This earth where we stand is the pure lotus land
And this very body, the body of Buddha."

– "Zazen Wasan" (Song of Zazen)
by Hakuin

Nowhere Is It Not

It is apparently body-wisdom that the Hippocratic Writings alluded to, two millennia ago, in stating that "there is a measure of conscious thought throughout the body."

Porphyry (c. 250 A.D.) was more specific, speaking of the intelligible ("which can not be enclosed in any place"—including the body):

> "The intelligible, therefore, is not imprisoned within the body; it spreads in all the body's parts, it penetrates them, it goes through them, and could not be enclosed in any *place.*"

This is an "intelligence" which goes beyond what we think of in connection with human consciousness. It is the essential intelligence which permits the brain to operate, whether or not "consciousness" is present.

Thus noted Larry Dossey, M.D.:

> "If we take consciousness seriously, we are faced with the conundrum that nobody has succeeded in registering its existence in an experiment. That is to say, the human brain has been much explored, and a great deal of its workings understood; but so far it has not been experimentally demonstrated that consciousness is needed as an additional component in the operation of the brain."

It is this "beyond the body" essence that he describes as a "nonlocal," or unitary, "mind":

> "The nonlocal view suggests that the mind cannot be limited to specific points in space (brains or bodies)

324

or in time (the present moment), but is infinite in space and time; thus the mind is omnipresent, eternal, and immortal. If minds are indeed nonlocal, this means that in principle they cannot be walled off and separated from one another: at some level they are unitary and one."

And physicist Erwin Schrödinger put it in this succinct perspective: "Mind by its very nature is a *singulare tantum*. I would say the overall number of minds is just one."

We would not assume that, say, a bar magnet has a "mind of its own," nor a consciousness per se; neither would we ascribe to "its intelligence" that it unerringly maintains a positive polarity at one end of the bar and a constant negative polarity at its other end. But there is something about the essence of such a "lifeless" piece of metal that permits us to break it in two anywhere and it will instantly reassert its positive/negative polarities at the proper, respective ends of each of the newly-severed pieces.

Physicist Fritjof Capra has noted, "When we magnify a 'dead' piece of stone or metal, we see that it is full of activity. The closer we look at it, the more alive it appears."

The sage who allegedly commented "before Abraham, *I am*," Jesus, is quoted in the *Gospel of Thomas*: "Cleave a piece of wood, I am there; lift up the stone, and you will find me there."

Here is the exceedingly subtle, but vital, aspect of the Absolute that is difficult to elucidate—and which terms like energy and intelligence tend to complicate: it is not that there is a universal mind (or intelligence, or cosmic consciousness) that governs the behavior of the bar magnet:

it is that all things are *intrinsically* "self-directing." And even the term *self-directing* is inadequate.

The "essence" of which we speak is not a property, which has a locus: being truly *essence-tial*, it is an actuality which is ubiquitous. Put another way, it is not a "universal" intelligence which emanates from a central cosmic mind, or consciousness; it is an omnipresent essence ("fundamental nature") which is—if there could be any such thing—the cosmic mind in its entirety.

It is a "mind" entirely devoid of any limitation whatsoever. Absolute. Formless.

Not only is this difficult to elucidate, but particularly in its entirety. But let us examine further.

Capra says in discussing so-called virtual particles (short-lived, in practical effect), "all material particles 'self-interact' by emitting and reabsorbing virtual particles... virtual particles can come into being spontaneously out of the void, and vanish again into the void...formed out of nothing." A single particle, by itself, "may very well emit a virtual particle, and reabsorb it shortly afterwards."

Capra says that "all material particles self-interact" in this way. Stephen Hawking says that in the region of the universe that we can observe, alone, there are approximately "1-with-eighty-zeroes-after-it particles." That would keep a *centralized* "Universal-Mind" agency busy, wouldn't it?

And if that were not enough to keep the agency switchboard lit up, consider this: A centimeter is about 4/10 of an inch: divide that into a million parts, then parse one of those parts into 100 slivers; that could be the width of an atom. Now reduce that atom by about 100,000 times, and that's the size of its nucleus. This nucleus represents 99.9 % of the atom's entire mass! Herein reside protons and neutrons; and something "informs" them to race about at approximately twenty percent of the speed of light.

There are an awful lot of atoms which would need to be thus informed. Take an average orange, for instance. Expand it to the size of our earth (about 8,000 miles wide). Stuff this 8,000-mile-wide orange full of cherries, and you have the approximate number of atoms...that are in *one orange*. A central intelligence agency would have an immense amount of informing, and governing to do from *afar*; it would be considerably more "intelligent" to simply inform, or govern, at every site.

This arrangement, whereby Intelligence *has no center*, is not so curious as it might seem. Not only is it everywhere that there is, but it is *always* so. Having always been so, it is not as if it "happened" onto the scene: nor even that it "created" the scene; it is the scene. Therefore it is not arduously at its task, working *against* something: there is not anything which is not already informed by its presence. So it has made matters exceedingly simple for itself!

One of the labor-saving devices of this ubiquitous essence, or Intelligence, is simultaneity. Where all things occur at the same time, one need not occupy oneself with such concerns as "cause" and "effect." Therefore there need be no central agency, in command at a switchboard: given instantaneous simultaneity, there would be "no time" for distantly-communicated directions to be carried out. "On-site management" would be the only practicality.

This is what the philosopher Ludwig Wittgenstein apparently meant when he said of *eternity* that it is "not infinite temporal duration, but timelessness." Not "time ever-lasting," but the utter absence of time. And so, this Intelligence, being eternal, has no constraints in—or relationships to—the duration of time. The entirety of its information is always wholly present to itself, being itself omnipresent.

As an old Zen master put it, "the one Mind, beside which nothing exists...is spontaneously existing." Alan Watts said of Eastern wisdom, "The moment of the world's creation is seen to lie not in some unthinkably remote past, but in the eternal now." Thomas Aquinas reportedly stated very clearly:

> "God does not move at all, and so cannot be measured by time; neither does He exist 'before or after', or no longer exist after having existed; nor can any succession be found in Him...but has the whole of His existence simultaneously; and that is the nature of eternity."

If one is incapable of discerning the implications of the infinite and timeless, the phenomenal nature of Absolute intelligence could scarcely be apprehended. Rene Guenon put it this way:

> "He who cannot escape from the standpoint of temporal succession, so as to see all things in their simultaneity, is incapable of the least conception of the metaphysical order."

Absolute intelligence would have to be entirely unrestrained by time and distance—or it would in no way be absolute. Therefore, there could be no time nor place where it was not always already present. This is the *meaning* of "Omnipresence."

But the most difficult aspect of this for people to grasp is that it is always *wholly present* in its Absolute *entirety* wherever it is. (And you'll recall where *that* is.) No "parts."

Wilber states it thus, "the *whole* of the infinite can be present in all points of space; for being itself spaceless, it does not contend with space; [and more importantly,] the entire Absolute is completely and wholly present at every point of space and time, for the simple reason that you can't have a different infinite at each point."

In summary, Wilber on this important aspect: "That, simply, is the meaning of omnipresence—the Absolute is simultaneously present everywhere and everywhen *in its entirety*."

With this pivotal understanding, it is possible to plumb further depths. Sublime intelligence not only has no need for a center, but would be encumbered by such. Therefore, all parts are *autonomously* intelligent, or self-directing. No "part," or element, in the universe, in other words, is "more central" or more *important* than any *other* part: all are *wholly* equal.

Says Capra: "The principal schools of Eastern mysticism thus agree...that the universe is an interconnected whole, in which no part is any more fundamental than the other..." He cites as physicist David Bohm's view that "the whole being is enfolded in each of its parts"; as earlier, Sir Charles Eliot stated, "each object in the world is not merely itself but involves every other object, and in fact is everything else."

Physicist Nick Herbert is even more specific about this, at the bare subatomic level:

> "The mechanism for this instant connectedness is not some invisible field that stretches from one part to the next, but the fact that a bit of each part's 'being' is lodged in the other. Each quon leaves some of its 'phase' *in the other's care*, and this phase exchange connects them *forever after*."

To "leave some of its phase" translates as sharing in common its information, or, more properly, intelligence. This could be read, "a bit of each part's 'essence' is lodged in the other."

Any wonder, then, that Huang Po understood the "holographic" universe long before the word was coined?

> "The essential Buddha-nature is a perfect whole, without superfluity or lack. It permeates the finite realms of existence and yet remains everywhere completely whole. Thus, every single one of the myriads of phenomena in the universe is the absolute."

Physicist Erwin Schrödinger:

> "Inconceivable as it seems to ordinary reason, you— and all other conscious beings as such—are all in all. Hence this life of yours which you are living is not merely a *piece* of the entire existence, but is in a certain sense the *whole*...."

And Garma Chang could hardly be more explicit:

> "In the infinite Dharmadhatu, each and every thing simultaneously includes all (other things) in perfect

completion, without the slightest deficiency or omission, at all times. To see one object is, therefore, to see all objects, and vice versa. This is to say, a tiny individual particle within the minute cosmos of an atom actually contains the infinite objects and principles, in the infinite universes of the future and of the remote past, in perfect completeness without omission."

"The mechanism for this instant [simultaneous] connectedness," as Herbert puts it, is that there is no "part" that is without the *same* intelligence, or essence, as every other "part."

In other words, the intelligence in (that is, of) each "thing" directly informs the intelligence of each other things. You may call it a "phase exchange" if you like, or resort to the simple phrase "all in all." All those cherries packed in that gigantic orange are in contact, in "touch" with each other; if they were steel marbles, and you applied sufficient electrical energy, you could touch any one of them and discover that they are all shockingly "alive." That "energy" is really their "essence," and all things "share" it commonly: it is the "one Mind," a mind that can be said to be in "perfect completion without omission"—Absolute.

Capra says it thus:

> "In the new view, the universe is seen as a dynamic web of interrelated events. None of the properties of any part of this web is fundamental, *they all follow from the properties of the other parts.*"

How *new* is that "new view"? The *I Ching* speaks of the universe as "without fixed law....It is only change that is at work here." In a universe where there is only change, fixed laws and immutable principles are superfluous.

Physicist Capra:

> "Physicists have come to see that all their theories of natural phenomena, including the 'laws' they describe, are creations of the human mind; properties of our conceptual map of reality, rather than of reality itself....

> "The 'bootstrap hypothesis' not only denies the existence of fundamental constituents of matter, but accepts *no fundamental entities whatsoever—no fundamental laws, equations or principles*—and thus abandons another idea which has been an essential part of natural science for hundreds of years. The notion of fundamental 'laws' of nature was derived from the belief in a Divine law*giver...*"

A self-actualizing intelligence needs no outward directives or laws. Astrophysicist Paul Davies states plainly: "It is no longer necessary to assume that the organization of the world requires an organizing *agency to create it* in a special condition."

As a consequence, physicist Steven Weinberg has said: "... the more we know about the universe, the more it is evident that it is pointless and meaningless."

His evident thrust is that in a holographic universe, which is not governed from afar by a centralized law-enforcement agency, there is no point from which a specific or particular meaning emanates. Any notion of autocratic governance, from the top down, is a contradiction of an Intelligence which is itself *illimitable.* The point is, for those who might consider this pointless, all things have *equal* meaning, *none* more fundamental than any other. It is the *same* essence which imbues all that is. This is what is meant, in Buddhism, by: "the one is seen as *pervading* them all and at the same time *embracing* them all in itself."

For that reason, the Buddhist scholar D.T. Suzuki cautions us that "this conception of great Source as existing separately somewhere is the fundamental mistake we all make..."

It is not that there is a great Source "somewhere" *out there* which has the capacity to diffuse or de-centralize. It is that there is an essence which pertains simultaneously at every point and instant—an *unbroken,* indivisible whole. If somehow this sounds remarkably simple, it *is*—in the sense that *simple* means "having only one part or feature."

Having only one part or property, the entire cosmic ball of wax—jointly and severally—is always everywhere entirely autonomous, or autogenetic. Call it self-interacting, self-consistent, self-completing, self-determinate (or, as physicists do, indeterminate), the point is that it is wholly all-in-all. To use Wilber's phrase, "...it is *in* the visible, yet invisible; *in* the divisible, yet indivisible."

Capra states: "An indivisible universe, in which all things and events are interrelated, would hardly make sense unless it were self-consistent."

His colleague, physicist Geoffrey Chew, has said, "Consciousness...is necessary for self-consistency of the whole." He evidently does not mean, however, a separate, isolated, centralized consciousness, but rather essential, "on-site" Intelligence.

This is a self-consistent intelligence which emanates from no locus (other than its "self"—and *all things* are its self), from no "center," and therefore has no "direction"—other than its self-direction. "God is a sphere whose center is everywhere and whose circumference is nowhere." "While it is nowhere, nowhere is it not." "Who sees not God everywhere, sees him nowhere."

Being omnipresent, infinite, timeless, this essence is not in "relationship" to anything, in terms of here/there, before/after, or cause/effect.

Thus Wilber says:

> That is to say, the Godhead's "actions" are without purpose or goal, effort or volition, motive or desire, cause or effect—for all of that implies a future aim and God knows no future or past, but only an Eternal Now.

We are not only "in" this eternal Presence, this Presence is "in" us—as in all things. It is not "outside" of us, or away or apart from us, except to the extent that it is the Presence of all things.

Say the Upanishads of this ever-present intelligence, this sublime essence:

> It is far, and It is near.
> It is within all this,
> And It is outside of all this.

No Program

Yes, as you indicated; the end of the road for all spiritual teachings is the *absence* of teachings.

For that matter, the end of the road for spiritual teachings is the absence of every*thing*.

It is difficult for those who are looking at these matters to comprehend the full import of what "oneness" means.

Where there is *only* one thing—which is what "oneness" *means*—there cannot possibly be any distinctions, under any circumstances. Therefore, given that situation, no word, concept or idea has any validity whatsoever: all *that* requires multiplicity.

Consider: when you die, this is exactly the circumstance which likely prevails.

Fortunately, we have the capacity to realize, while we are *alive*, that *ultimately* nothing really matters. Considering that, ultimately *nothing* really matters, how much anguish should we invest in our temporal, impermanent, "relative" fixations in the meantime?

One of the reasons I highly regard Ramana as exemplary is that he lived his life as an instructive answer to that question. If one puts as little energy into relating to this world as he did, would one be unwise?

In my estimation, any teaching which assists one to connect with the reality of the sheer emptiness of their existence— in life or death—is a practical teaching.

When this connection to the impersonal noumenon is made, "you" evaporate, teachers evaporate, teaching evaporates. Not anything can remain, not even that which points to That.

Krishnamurti stated that his imperative—the role of the true spiritual exponent—was "to set man absolutely, unconditionally free." Would a person who is "absolutely, unconditionally free" not be free of an attachment to the teacher, and free ultimately of any bondage to the teachings which connected that person to a teacher?

The object of truly spiritual teachings, surely, is not to create a follower of orthodoxy, whose behavior is predictably mechanical or reactive. Robotic compulsion can in no fashion be equated with freedom. Spiritual freedom would suggest an atmosphere for creative, spontaneous action, rather than attachment to patterns and traditions and a program of "do's" and "don'ts."

In other words, consider that the essence of spiritual teachings is not founded upon an intention to instruct one in how to comport oneself in the future, but rather in the necessity of one's *total attention* in this unending moment that is the *present*. This is what it means to be unconditioned, to be deprogrammed, or—at the very least, to be "programmatically divergent."

You are the teacher; you are your teaching; *and* you are the taught. The ultimate teaching is that, ultimately, there is no teaching.

Therefore, from the standpoint of this understanding, *no* teachings are indispensable: all that any of them can tell you is that, in the comprehension of "oneness," there is no "individual" remaining who needs to be taught.

Ultimate reality is, by definition,
   present everywhere and everywhen.

Being beginningless and endless in time and space,
   infinite Presence is formless.

Forms, material or immaterial, arise and subside
   within eternal Presence.

Limitless Presence surrounds and permeates all
   forms.

Infusing the "many," this omnipresence constitutes
   One indivisible actuality.

Every event and activity, positive or negative, is
   a manifestation of this ground of Be-ing—
   including *all* thoughts and actions, yours and
   others'.

Every form (alive or lifeless) and occurrence
   (inward or outward) is a component—"good,"
   "bad," or otherwise—of the originating Source.

Realizing this is called awakening.

For the awakened, thoughts, feelings and actions
   are viewed as unmitigated expressions of
   flawless reality.

Contact

Robert Wolfe
robert@livingnonduality.org

c/o Karina Library Press
PO Box 35
Ojai, CA 93024

To support the reach of Robert's work:
www.livingnonduality.org/donate

For free text, audio, and video materials:
www.livingnonduality.org

Leave a review, and help others discover this work:
www.livingnonduality.org/reviews

Alphabetical Title Index

Made in the USA
San Bernardino, CA
28 December 2015